THE
PROMISE

THE
PROMISE

GOD'S PURPOSE AND PLAN
FOR WHEN LIFE HURTS

FATHER JONATHAN MORRIS

Fox News Faith & Value Correspondent

HarperOne
An Imprint of HarperCollinsPublishers

HarperOne

THE PROMISE: *God's Purpose and Plan for When Life Hurts.* Copyright © 2008 by Father Jonathan Morris. All rights reserved. Printed in the United States of America. No part of this book may be used or reproduced in any manner whatsoever without written permission except in the case of brief quotations embodied in critical articles and reviews. For information address HarperCollins Publishers, 10 East 53rd Street, New York, NY 10022.

HarperCollins books may be purchased for educational, business, or sales promotional use. For information please write: Special Markets Department, HarperCollins Publishers, 10 East 53rd Street, New York, NY 10022.

HarperCollins Web site: http://www.harpercollins.com

HarperCollins®, ▤®, and HarperOne™ are trademarks of HarperCollins Publishers

FIRST EDITION

The names of the people discussed in this book have been changed to protect their privacy.

Library of Congress Cataloging-in-Publication Data is available.
ISBN: 978–0–06–135341–3

08 09 10 11 12 RRD(H) 10 9 8 7 6 5 4 3 2 1

I dedicate this book to you, the reader.

My prayer is that these pages will help you experience—like never before—deep inner peace and joy, even in the midst of great pain.

CONTENTS

Contents

THE
PROMISE

INTRODUCTION

Stand by; we're coming to you, Father . . .
five, four, three, two . . .

At Fox News we were dealing with back-to-back natural disasters. Who could forget the video images of the arrival and the aftermath of the Asian tsunami—three hundred thousand dead? Little time passed before the earth quaked in Pakistan and swallowed seventy-three thousand hardworking people already struggling for survival. The same year reporters documented in real time the overnight transformation of New Orleans, one of America's most beloved cities, into a ghost town.

The television anchor who was about to interview me was a good guy—straitlaced and professional. As far as I knew he was not particularly religious. We were scheduled to talk about charity and international aid.

But today he couldn't help himself, and he dropped the bomb: "People are wondering what's behind all this death and destruction, all at one time. Tell me, is God ticked off?"

The question hung there across the airways and in my head. He wanted me to answer the oldest and hardest question of humankind—whether God is responsible for what we suffer—and he wanted me to do so live, on national television, and in thirty seconds or less.

I can't remember exactly how I responded to the pointed question in that interview. But for the next few months, I couldn't get the anchor's question out of my head. Of course, as a man of the cloth, I was familiar with the subject of God and suffering, and how they can coexist. In seminary I had studied all the books and had convinced myself I had it all worked out—at least on an intellectual level.

But all of a sudden I knew I didn't. Behind this anchor's honest and spontaneous question I imagined throngs of other people calling to me through their television screens. At the end of the day, they cared much less about the particular issue of whether we can blame God for natural disasters and more about how to get rid of the suffering—or at least how to rediscover inner peace and meaning in the midst of darkness. Life had taught me that mere theoretical musings from the classroom do not work when people are hurting; in fact, hurting people are often insulted when all they hear are textbook answers.

But whatever the nature of our question, when we watch the news, we all make one deduction: life is hard—for humanity in general, and for me in particular. In fact, for some it really stinks.

Is that the way it's supposed to be?

When we were kids they told us about a God who is all-loving, all-powerful, and who knows us—even the number of hairs on our head—and wants the best for us.

Then we grew up.

Now we ask, at some point or another, how to reconcile in our minds the existence of such a good and strong God with a world where everyone hurts. We want to put God on trial. Some point a finger at God out of bitterness; they want vengeance for what seem like broken promises. However, most people I know who ask these tough questions still have sparks of faith, and they hope there is an explanation; they just have no idea what it is.

Introduction

This book is meant to help you understand why, if God exists, he seems not to care. But above all, this book is intended to help you suffer less by helping you learn to suffer better—with meaning and purpose—and thus be free to experience peace and happiness as you've never experienced them before. Is this really possible? It is. I've experienced this process in my own life, and I've witnessed it in the lives of many others. This book is full of real-life examples.

My goal is to provide something to know and something to live—to address both your mind and your heart. I have not written a textbook answer to the philosophical question of suffering and evil; rather, this is a guidebook of spiritual principles and practical ideas—examples and techniques, rooted in the teachings and the person of Jesus of Nazareth—that aim to *better your life*.

This book has three parts. The first part is about who God is and who he isn't. Since we are supposed to trust God with our pain and suffering, we had better know who we are supposed to trust. Part 1 is thus dedicated to the renewal of the mind. Part 2 is a roadmap to spiritual and emotional healing. Suffering is not about something that hurt once and from which we then recover. I have found that suffering has psychological and spiritual consequences that need to be addressed and healed, and not just explained away. In part 3, I offer a set of life-affirming principles to live by that can teach us to find true freedom in the midst of a world that is hurting. Finally, I have included supplementary material, in the form of three appendices, that explores the core theological and philosophical explanations for how God could allow everyone to hurt so much and still be a loving and good God. To make sure this material does not get overly theoretical, I have written it as a series of fictitious dialogues between Dr. Woods, a theologian, and Vanessa, a mother who has experienced the worst possible crime—the abuse and murder of her child.

A Note About Me

I have a day job and a night job. By day, I do what many pastors and priests—and moms and dads—do; I listen to the struggles, victories, joys, and sorrows of others and try to help each person discover his path to personal fulfillment.

By night I do something quite different: I give live television commentary, from an ethical perspective, on the big news stories of the day. While the appearance of my work changes, the story line stays the same. The personal drama suffered in the privacy of our own homes is eerily similar to what we see on the television screen—tragedy, broken relationships, partisan bickering, betrayal, poverty, disease, sadness, and so much more.

I've dedicated most of my ministry as a priest to one-on-one counseling—giving spiritual direction to young people, married couples, business professionals, and the sick. I've tried to listen, listen, and listen, and then help them discern God's plan for their personal freedom and fulfillment. Their pain has made me cry with them at times, always laugh with them, and finally search for down-to-earth answers that are true and that satisfy.

This book is based on biblical principles, but it is not just for fervent Christians. It is for all of us who are looking for sense in suffering and who are open to answers even if they come from sources we thought were old-fashioned and passé.

You will notice that many of my suggestions for how to discover or recover joy in the midst of suffering can be followed by anyone, even people without the gift of faith.

For those of you who possess the gift of faith, I hope to help you face what and why we believe. Faith matters only if it coincides with truth. That's why I have done my best not to sugarcoat the power of suffering. I've tried to give suffering a fair shake. Christian bookstores are full of treatises that defend the faith, and that's a good thing. But this book is not a defense. I'm sharing with you what I have learned from personal experience and from others about what *works* when it comes to living with suffering, and *why* it does.

I also want to confront the fact that faith alone is not a solution to our pain. I know many people of great faith who are a mess, emotionally and spiritually, and don't know why. Like everyone else, we Christians have wounds. This book is also about healing the inner wounds that block us from experiencing true freedom.

Finally, I hope our expedition into the problem of suffering will help Christians help others. It will give you the tools to talk graciously and effectively with family and friends who see suffering as an insurmountable obstacle to faith in God.

How to Use This Book

Just as our suffering usually develops in stages, each building on the other, I have seen that the journey to inner peace and meaning generally follows a certain order. The order isn't the same for everyone, but the one I am presenting here represents the way I have seen God work most often in people's lives. Each part of this book leads into the next, but you may want to jump to those sections that are most relevant to what you are currently dealing with. In fact, you may wish to read only those.

At the end of the book, there are three appendices that serve as supplementary material for the reader who wishes to explore more deeply the core theological and philosophical explanations for how God could allow every one to suffer so much and still be a loving and good God.

At the end of each chapter and appendix, I offer some points for personal reflection or discussion. They function as a summary of the chapter or appendix's main points and a launching pad for personal reflection. Some may wish to read this book as a group project. Gather a group of friends or coworkers. Read one or two chapters, and then answer the questions or make up your own.

Dispersed throughout are letters addressed to me from people who knew I was writing this book and wanted to tell me their stories. They are labeled in the text as "From My In-box." I think they put a needed face on suffering. They keep us down to earth. For the sake of privacy, I have changed these people's names and other identifying elements of their stories. For the purpose of clarity, I've also created some composite characters by meshing real stories from various people's lives into the life of one.

PART ONE

GOD ON TRIAL

1

Do You Even Care, God?

Cast all your worries upon him because he cares for you.

—I PETER 5:7

When a mother kisses the cut on her son's scraped knee and promises, "This will make it go away," she isn't telling a pious fib. Her presence, in her lips and in her words, truly heals the hurt.

The Scriptures say that God is love (1 John 4:8), but when it comes to someone being there for us when we suffer, it seems our earthly mother is a whole lot more reliable than our heavenly Father.

Where is God when we need him most?

A story from the Gospel of Mark explains beautifully one of the key elements of the Christian theology of suffering: God is with us.

If you want to understand Christianity, if you want to understand—or rather to know—Jesus Christ, this is a good place to start. You aren't so sure you believe that a two-thousand-year-old

9

story has anything to do with your pain? That's understandable. For now, I invite you to just listen in.

Jesus is traveling across the sea with his disciples after an evening of preaching to the crowds. He decides to catch up on some sleep while his disciples, seamen by trade, tend to the navigation. Little by little night falls, the breeze builds, a light shower becomes a downpour, and the waves gain strength. Unexpectedly the travelers find themselves in the midst of a violent squall while the rush of cold seawater mercilessly swamps their little boat.

They skate across the deck and holler between themselves, futilely trying to keep their humble vessel afloat. But all is in vain, and they know it. Hope is cast away and swallowed up in the tempest. Where is God in all this?

> *Jesus was in the stern, asleep on a cushion. They woke him and said to him, "Teacher, do you not care that we are perishing?" (Mark 4:38)*

In other words, "Of course you don't care, or you wouldn't be in the back of the boat. Do you really think we believe you're sleeping in the middle of a squall?"

Frustration and fear are in that question, but also grief: "We're dying! Don't you *care?*" That would be the real horror. Maybe God just doesn't care. Maybe all our pleas just fall on deaf ears.

The disciples asked this for the rest of humanity. All eyes are on Jesus. All ears are waiting on his word. The disciples said their piece. They expressed their gripes plain and clear. They accused Jesus, the divine Son of God, of indifference. Can't you just see the nameless disciple with soaked hair pasted to his forehead, glaring into Jesus' eyes as if to say, "Anything to say for yourself, Teacher?"

> *He woke up, rebuked the wind, and said to the sea, "Quiet!*
> *Be still!" The wind ceased and there was great calm.*
> *Then he asked them, "Why are you terrified? Do you not*
> *yet have faith?"*
> *They were filled with great awe and said to one another,*
> *"Who then is this whom even wind and sea obey?"*
> *(Mark 4:39–41)*

The most compelling part of this Gospel story is that it is true. It really happened: the man who calmed the seas and who claimed to be divine submitted himself to the same tumultuous waves as the mortals who complained. The narration mirrors our posture before God and his before us. It unveils our ignorance, self-centeredness, and lack of trust. In the face of threatening troubles we question God's power; we doubt his goodness. The God whose blessings we were counting brief moments before is now the target of our pointing finger.

Kim was a real-estate agent with a handsome husband named Jim, who made a good living selling corporate insurance. He had a membership at the country club, and he and their three boys were into sailing. Winter vacation was often spent in Naples, Florida, where they held a timeshare. Private school for the kids, K through 12, was a given. Life was good and fast, but, on top of their busy schedules, they usually squeezed in time for church on Sundays. They weren't religious fanatics, and from what I remember they were proud of that, too. Religion was a cultural thing and served the good purpose of teaching moral principles to the kids and calming what would otherwise be guilt-ridden parental consciences.

In other words, faith was something they did, not lived.

Kim was zipping down the Van Wyck Expressway on her way to pick up Jim at Kennedy Airport one Saturday morning. The Land Cruiser suddenly stalled, and she slowed to a stop on the shoulder. As she huffed and sheepishly went to lift the hood, she managed a nervous laugh. *What do I know about cars?* she thought. Puzzled and anxious, she cupped her face into her hands and then looked down to see the cars passing beneath her: she was on the overpass. Then came the crash.

An eighteen-wheeler collided with her back bumper and catapulted Kim to the perpendicular freeway stories below. The first speeding cars managed to dodge her body. When emergency vehicles arrived on the scene they found her alive, barely.

Kim was transported to a nearby hospital, where—days later, when she came to—she learned she had fractured fourteen bones and suffered a concussion. The doctors informed her husband that she wouldn't be leaving anytime soon.

The suffering had just begun. Kim was in a full-body cast and virtually immobilized. That would be her story for the next twelve weeks. Beyond that, since the moment she awoke, she was in excruciating pain, and no medicine seemed to offer any relief. Jim was beside himself that the doctors couldn't ease her suffering. All he could do was keep her company. The rest of the family did the same, taking long and wearisome shifts.

During one rare moment, neither Jim nor any of the kids were by her side. A family member of a patient in a neighboring room noticed the empty room and stopped in just to say hello. She spontaneously asked Kim if she would like to pray with her. Kim didn't respond. (She had never prayed with anyone.) The woman took the silence as tacit permission to pray out loud. Kim certainly didn't mind the company, and the rhythm of the prayer brought back good memories from her childhood, when her grandmother used to pray out on the davenport. No more than a few minutes into the prayers, Kim realized that her pain was somehow less.

Kim and her guest finished just as Jim arrived. Kim managed a wink of gratitude in the direction of her new friend. Half an hour later she confided her secret to Jim. He wiped her forehead with a washcloth and tried to help her rest, but he didn't understand her new discovery.

Kim's pain slowly returned. This time, however, it felt different. When she couldn't bear it anymore, she asked the next relative on shift to pray those same prayers with her. Kim stumbled through the words, waiting for something to happen. Over time, she began uniting her heart to the meaning of each word. The prayer was becoming personal, felt. It was hers. The pressure in her head began to subside, and she could now breathe more easily. She also smiled regularly at Jim, and he now understood that although she wasn't wholly well, from one day to the next she was getting better.

The nurse who tended to Kim asked what it was that was making her feel better. "I talk to God," Kim explained. "Honey," said the nurse in a thick Brooklyn accent as she changed the bedpan, "whatever works!" By this time Kim knew that what was happening was not "mind over matter," as the nurse surmised. The power did not come from inside her; it came from God. The prayer shifts became a regular family event for weeks to come, and though the praying may have started out as something of a lucky charm, the inexplicable results invited the family members to examine their own faith.

Jim started paying attention when the Baptist minister and Catholic priest would make their rounds. Their oldest son, Jim Jr., asked to make his confirmation that year. Their third-grader took more interest in religion classes. They all opened their souls to the blessings of God.

When Kim tells this story, she says God never looked the other way. His silence during the accident itself and the days that followed was not indifference. He suffered with her, and patiently waited for her to go to him in his apparent slumber and to ask him the tough question: "Teacher, do you not care that we are perishing?" Looking back on the first weeks of her recovery, she says the slumber had not been his, but hers. Jesus awoke and calmed her sea.

Humbly, he wakes to that pointing finger.

FROM MY IN-BOX

I used to believe. I used to pray. No more. Everything I had, everything I loved—I've lost it all. Who needs a God who only cares for a time, who runs and hides when things get rough? Is he hiding a smirk, a mean smile that mocks the power I thought he had?

—*Susie*

Pope John Paul II, a man loved not only by Catholics, knew suffering from the inside. He was left without relatives by the age of twenty-one, survived the horrors of Nazi and Communist regimes, was shot by an attempted assassin, and then lived his last years stricken by humbling infirmity in the public's eye. In *Crossing the Threshold of Hope,* he explains God's role in suffering this way: "God is always on the side of the suffering."

Did the disciples not think of that? Why don't we? Instead, we point the finger as we moan, "Why me?" We assume that we suffer alone, when in fact Jesus suffers with us. He's in our corner; he's in the room. When Jesus takes account of the situation—the furious waves, the fallen sails—he does not crumble into a frantic wreck. He knows whose hands are in control and that we are in the safekeeping of those hands. The security he has in his Father is indomitable. His sleep is not like ours.

When Jesus works a miracle, as he did on the boat with the disciples or in Kim's hospital room, he does it to show that his power is unabated.

When he rises from the hull and speaks, his command is to the sea, but it applies also to us: "'Quiet! Be still!' The wind ceased and there was great calm."

At the sound of Jesus' words, rebel winds subside, and in their awe the disciples feel small. Small, but big, because they now know they're not alone, and never were.

There are people out there, in our own neighborhoods, who live this living faith every day.

FROM MY IN-BOX

When bad things happen, some people turn away from God. But I turn to him and he makes me strong. I've lost my mom, two grandparents, and my brother all within the past four years. All the while, God was there. And although I have never seen a reason for my brother's untimely death, I know that there is a purpose. I love the Lord.

—*Mike*

Kim's story will make a lot of sense to readers who already believe in the power of God and his regular intervention in human affairs. They can easily assume that something supernatural really happened, because their personal experience and faith tell them that Kim's story is not an isolated happening.

But before the accident Kim would not have been this type of reader. She would have attributed the healing to psychological or circumstantial factors. Or more likely, she would have avoided the question altogether, aware that there are lots of things in life we don't understand. In Kim's old playbook, this would be just another mystery—happily, a positive one. In her new playbook, the one initiated by an experience of the presence of God in her life, the healing was God's way of saying he really does care. A person of faith like Kim believes that God sometimes expresses his personal care and love through healing while at other times he chooses other means.

The story of Jesus calming the sea, however, is ultimately what explains Kim's story to the rest of us, especially those who have never been healed, never witnessed a miracle.

Christians believe that Jesus is divine, that he is the Son of God, the second person of the Holy Trinity. So did the disciples, in their own escalating way. That's why they rightly turned to him and wondered why he wasn't intervening. They sound a little bit like us: "God, if you are who you say you are, why do you hide?"

This question presupposes that the best thing for them and us is to never experience choppy seas. Jesus' own words tell us that this is not so. "Why are you terrified? Do you not yet have faith?" The faith Jesus asks about is not only faith in his power to calm whitecaps. It is about faith in the big picture. What if the boat were to go under? What if they were to suffer or even to die in this turbulent sea? Could Jesus, the Son of God, not bring out a greater good even from that?

The disciples came out of this trial better for the wear. Kim did, too. Isn't this what often happens to us? Although we wouldn't choose to go through trauma all over again, we would be hesitant to exchange the blessings we've gained through what we've undergone. Good from evil: this is the first glimpse of some sense in suffering. It is part of God's response to human suffering.

There are other cases, of course, where it is impossible to find proportion between what we've gained and what we've lost. Trust in Jesus means accepting that his will for our life is perfect, even when it is different from our idea of a good plan. He doesn't chide the disciples for fighting the seas. He doesn't suggest they roll over and play dead. They do the right thing by using their heads, their skills, and all their natural talents to navigate the boat to more tranquil waters to avoid unnecessary suffering. But Jesus does call them to task for their lack of trust. He wants to teach them this lesson: If their life course is changed by an act of God—choppy seas—might not that, too, be part of God's bigger and better plan?

True faith believes in God's love even when God chooses not to intervene.

Questions for Personal Reflection or Discussion

➤ Does the evil I see or the suffering I experience move me toward God or away from God?

➤ Have I lost trust in God? If so, what were the causes?

2

Reasonable Faith?

*Ever since the creation of the world, his invisible attributes of
eternal power and divinity have been able to be understood and
perceived in what he has made.*

—ROMANS 1:20

Let's take a step back away from the Gospel and even from
directly talking about suffering to lay an important foundation for the rest of our discussion: Is it *reasonable* to turn to
faith for answers about our pain?

We all have moments of doubt. In low moments we wonder
if faith might be just a man-made survival technique in a nasty,
senseless world. And if this world is senseless, then not even
human reason will find sense in suffering. But I think *faith* and
reason are both trustworthy sources of truth, and we can rely on
both of them in life's most difficult moments. Let me explain.

Is It True for You?

Nowadays, it's useless to talk about trustworthy sources of truth without first tackling the question of whether we can know if anything is true in the first place. In our postmodern society, we are told to respect other people's views. This, it appears, is the only universally accepted virtue.

But while people always deserve respect, ideas must earn it. Giving equal value to all ideas is a destructive philosophy called *relativism*. This worldview claims that truth is never permanent or absolute, that truth is completely subjective; that it's relative to times and places, persons and cultures; and that the only thing we can know for certain is that nothing is necessarily true.

This philosophy pervades many aspects of our contemporary culture. But if everything is relative, we should never waste time uttering an opinion. Every explanation I give and every suggestion I make in this book would be just as right or wrong as the next guy's. If truth is absolutely relative, there is no answer to the problem of suffering. In fact, there's really no such thing as a problem in the first place; everything just "is."

But like many seductive philosophies, relativism does reflect partial truths. Some things do "depend." Circumstances and conditions are important. Cultures and peoples should not all look alike. Not *everything* that is right for me is right for you.

But relativism goes wrong by rejecting the idea that some things are always *true* and should be defended, that some things are always *good* and should be applauded. But not only are some things universally good and true; some things are always and everywhere bad and false and should be rejected—slavery, sexual abuse, Nazi-style eugenics, and much more. Would anyone deny that personal freedom is good? Would anyone deny that killing the innocent is bad? Hard-core relativists do so because, once again, it always depends.

The good news is that in the end the philosophy of relativism destroys itself. A hard-core relativist will say that his philosophy is absolutely true and that anyone who disagrees with him is absolutely wrong. But according to his own logic, if something is true it is true only for the realist himself.

America is today—and has been from her first days—very much a country of believers. Eighty percent of Americans identify themselves as Christians, and 90 percent say they are followers of some religion. For them, the quest for sense in suffering most likely has been a spiritual one. Nevertheless, the whole community of sufferers—not just the religious—needs an answer, and God, in his wisdom, allows us to grasp part of the answer through the exercise of our minds.

We can certainly find some sense in suffering before opening the Bible or talking about martyrs or the cross of Christ. While I believe that the deepest answer is found only in the realm of faith, there are many clues available to us about the meaning of suffering and how best to live with it even before we tap into divine revelation.

Not long ago I collaborated on a Fox News Channel Easter special titled *The Passion: Facts, Fictions, and Faith*. Lauren Green hosted the show, and Clay Rawson was the executive producer. They did a great job of intertwining various points of view—Evangelical, Protestant, Catholic, and non-Christian—without falling into the common trap of presenting historic facts as mere opinion and therefore debatable. After two thousand years of human interference, there are certainly a lot of myths surrounding the life and death of Jesus, but this doesn't mean everything is up for grabs—as if belief in Jesus' existence itself were an act of blind, religious faith. The honest approach of the television special allowed viewers to see the relationship between facts, fiction, and faith with regard to the passion of Jesus.

One anthropologist interviewed in the special challenged this approach (perhaps inadvertently). He said on the show, "There are those who want to know and those who want to believe." He is setting reason up against faith. I think it's a big and common mistake. The world is not divided into believers and knowers. God doesn't want us believers to close off our minds. He wants us to use them, and when we do, we are actually preparing ourselves to grasp the content of faith in a complementary, not a contradictory, way.

So what can our reasoning and logic tell us about God's purpose and plan for our suffering when we look at literature, philosophy, and culture? What grains of truth (or distortions of the truth) about the subject do we hear from pop musicians, Hollywood, and ad campaigns? What about everyday experience? This type of rational reflection will be an integral part of this book.

As long as human beings interact, we will have disagreements, especially about these tough issues, and that's nothing to be scandalized about. But I think that if we learn to use both faith and reason better, our discussions will be more productive and we will be able to avoid falling into the tribal attitudes that are so common in the areas of politics and religion.

Reason Alone Is Not Enough

I wouldn't have traded a comfortable pair of Levi's and my Italian silk ties for a wardrobe of all black (and a splash of white) if I didn't think God was central to life's biggest issues. My ring finger remains bare because I have chosen to dedicate my life exclusively to loving God and making known the solution I find in him.

I remember an old friend from my college days—let's call him Dan—who once challenged me about my faith in God. Dan was an atheist—one of the many honest ones I know. He was always cheerful, very intelligent, social, athletic, and funny; we got along great. One day, over a cold beer or two, I asked him why he didn't believe in God, and I saw a side of him I had never seen before. His eyes turned cold and serious as he said, "If there is a God who is all-powerful and still lets little innocent babies get all the horrible diseases that babies get—deformations from fetal alcohol syndrome, Down's syndrome, you name it—I have no problem giving that kind of God the middle finger!" I was taken aback. It was a passionate response. His conclusion sounded horrible to me, and yet there was a certain nobility about it. He considered it *virtuous* to hate such a God. I now know there are many others out there like my friend Dan.

Dan presented me with a serious dilemma: How could I defend my idea of an infinitely good God in the midst of all this suffering? How could a good God let this happen? I didn't know how, and for me, that meant crisis.

The point here is not to tackle the question head-on, but rather to say that in our quest for inner peace and meaning in the midst of suffering, we're not going to leave God out of the equation. We have to confront what our faith in him is all about.

Pope John Paul II describes marvelously the relationship between faith and reason in the opening line of his encyclical letter *Fides et Ratio:* "Faith and reason are like two wings on which the human spirit rises to the contemplation of truth; and God has placed in the human heart a desire to know the truth."

For John Paul II, faith and reason aren't two mutually exclusive sources of light. When they are used well, they are both valid means of reaching the truth.

What is faith? Faith is knowledge, but it is secondhand knowledge. We believe because we trust our source. Another way to put it is that faith is thinking *with assent*.

What is reason? Reason is firsthand knowledge. It involves understanding by myself—no need to trust some other authority.

But in actuality, reason too usually involves thinking with assent. How do we who aren't astrophysicists know that our neighboring galaxy, Andromeda, is 2.5 million light years away? Isn't it because we read books? It would be fair to object, "But that's science. Good scientists with good instruments tell us things are as they are." And that's precisely the point: we assent to what they tell us because they are good scientists. We don't have to do the measuring ourselves. We don't verify the precision of each of their instruments and methods.

We don't have to talk rocket science to show that almost all of our knowledge has some element of faith. How do we know that George Washington walked the earth? Did we pick cherries with him? We assume that history books tell us the truth, but we can't back up what we read in them with firsthand experience.

Or take something as ordinary as getting directions from the guy in the subway. We follow his indications because, after sizing up what he looks like, how he's acting, and the assurance of his voice, we decide he knows what he's talking about.

Religious faith is similar, with one exception. It's not the guy in the subway we put our trust in, but rather God. And if he's God, then he's all-knowing, and he definitely knows what he's talking about. He can't deceive or be deceived: "A faithful God, without deceit, how just and upright he is!" (Deut. 32:4).

And what if I don't believe in God? would be a valid question here.

In a similar fashion, as we trust in multiple sources who tell us George Washington really walked the earth, we can find in nature, in the testimony of people we know, in history, and in personal experience plenty of *reasons* to believe. They point us in the direction of God. Because God chose to give us free will, he will never force us to believe. He will never disrespect our intellect by showing us "proof" of something supernatural. Instead, in his mysterious time line, God offers us the *gift* of faith.

Though it sometimes seems as if faith is contrary to reason because we don't understand a particular creed, the humble person recognizes that the problem may be with his own intellect. Our brains are only brains. They are small and limited.

On a final note, we can say faith and reason are mutually compatible because both have the same source: God. Reason is God's endowment to humanity. Man does not make reason; he only inherits it and discovers it. We assume reason is trustworthy because it "works." And it works because he fashioned it for a purpose. Within certain limits, it captures the reality of the world around us and the world within us: "Faith is the realization of what is hoped for and evidence of things not seen" (Heb. 11:1).

Faith, on the other hand, captures the realities beyond the reach of mere reason. It "works," too, having the same origin as reason. Faith is thinking not with my finite intellect—that's reason—but by adhering to the Infinite Intellect; for faith is assent to what is divinely revealed. That is why I believe faith is trustworthy, too— even more so than reason.

Humility invites us to trust that if God has said it, in due time—later on earth, or in heaven—we will see how the gift of faith perfectly coincides with God's first gift to us, our intellect and reason.

In summary, I would say it is not reasonable to be antifaith. It is reasonable to believe in more than what we can quantify through science. When we reject faith as a source of truth, we end up falling into the same dogmatic fundamentalism as those who empty faith of all its reason.

In *Fides et Ratio,* Pope John Paul II speaks to this point:

> *The fundamental harmony between the knowledge of faith*
> *and the knowledge of philosophy is once again confirmed.*
> *Faith asks that its object be understood with the help of reason,*
> *and at the summit of its searching, reason acknowledges that it*
> *cannot do without what faith presents.*

The explanation in this chapter doesn't "prove" that our notion of the Christian God is correct. I simply wanted to tear down some common prejudices that would have been crippling obstacles to any dialogue between faith and reason. I wanted to show that such a dialogue is possible—very possible!

In this book I'll continue to use explanations that originate in both reason and faith, in both natural and supernatural light. When we're in the dark about something as important as sense in suffering, I think it makes sense to use everything within our reach.

Questions for Personal Reflection or Discussion

➤ Do I think faith is reasonable? Am I able to explain this belief to others?

➤ Is learning more about God and my faith a priority in my life?

3

Someone Like God

I am the first and I am the last; there is no God but me.
Who is like me? Let him stand up and speak, make
it evident, and confront me with it.

—ISAIAH 44:6–7

I told you in chapter 1 not to worry if you didn't see the presence of Jesus on the ship as having much to say about your present pain. I said the doubt was understandable. This chapter and the next three will be dedicated to different aspects of this dilemma, beginning here with a review of misconceptions about who God is and of how these misconceptions distort our ability to accept the gift of faith, especially as it relates to our pain.

Not long ago I made mention of this same Gospel story in a published article. I received the following response from a reader:

> So he stopped a storm once, two thousand years ago—big deal! He doesn't calm the storms of my suffering now. I've

27

called out to him, I've tried to wake him up, but I'm living proof the guy doesn't answer prayers; he doesn't care. As far as I'm concerned, if God is still around, he's a jerk.

—*Adam*

Why do some people believe in God's power and willingness to intervene in our lives, and even say they have experienced his loving action, while others do not? An easy way out would be to say Adam just doesn't have the gift of faith and leave it at that. But I think there is more to it.

When Adam says he called out to God to wake him, to whom was he speaking? Whom did he try to wake?

In my experience, most vitriolic outbursts at the divine, like Adam's, have more to do with a misconception of who God is than a simple lack of faith. How can we expect to hear God's voice, feel his touch, or marvel at his miracles if we wouldn't recognize him even if he showed up in our living room?

Who is God? How does he act? What does he look like? As we have mentioned, America is still a highly religious country. We say we believe in God. But when we get down to brass tacks and try to describe who this divine being is and what he has to do with our lives, we may not have as much in common with each other or with the Christian faith as we might have thought.

I want to lead you through a few modern depictions of God. I am not going to offer a rebuttal to any of them. Just read along, and see if any of them reflects your own views, even in a partial way. Very few people fit squarely into any one particular view; however, each view influences the way we think and therefore the way we relate to God.

The theological arguments I offer in this book about how God wants to reach out to, bless, and heal those who are suffering make little sense if our idea of God is disfigured. We will always be falling back on false premises and blaming a "god" who doesn't exist.

In the coming chapters we will present the Christian God, and you will be able to see how he differs from the views of him that follow here.

God the Vending Machine

I remember visiting a couple in their mid-thirties in Connecticut who had been married for eight years. Like many other newlyweds, they had followed the contemporary "wisdom" that the best thing they could do for their marriage was to spend their first years as a married couple together and alone. So they enjoyed five years of two incomes and no children—eating out and traveling whenever they could. Then they decided to have kids. They bought a big house, settled down, and waited. No luck. By the time I met them—three years into the wait—Mary, the wife, was sad most of the time, weighed down by terrible guilt. Her husband, Mark, on the other hand, was just tired of all the doctor visits and the increasingly invasive and what he considered to be "dehumanizing" therapies to which they (especially Mary) had submitted themselves, at the various doctors' recommendations.

Mary and Mark hadn't been to church in years but were thrilled to have a priest visit their home. They lapped up every word about God and miracles. They asked for prayers. I suggested we pray that God's will be done in their lives—that God allow Mary to become pregnant if that is what he wanted for them. I didn't realize how strange my words would sound to them. "Pray that God's will be done?" "What?!" "We just want a baby!" I tried to explain what was behind my prayer approach, but from their blank stares I felt

I might as well have been talking to them in Latin. We prayed together anyway.

Admittedly I too felt disappointed when I left their house that night. They wanted desperately for me to help them achieve their objective, but for my part I couldn't promise anything. God isn't a vending machine.

When we don't receive an instant response to our suffering, we assume the God machine is broken. We press the buttons harder, just in case, and hit the coin return to get our money back. *Hellooo! I'm calling you, God! I'm praying, just like you told me to! How come you're not home?*

Several years later I ran into some of Mary and Mark's friends, who told me how the couple had adopted two Chinese children and were doing very well. In fact, Mary and Mark were very active members in the local church. It was only after coming to know and love their new children that they realized how God's will had been worked out in their lives. They couldn't imagine life without their two children, ones they would not have had if their initial desires had been fulfilled. They saw how the strange prayer we prayed together, the one they didn't understand, wasn't so strange after all. God's will, not theirs, came to fruition, and it turned out to be a perfect fulfillment for them.

God the Clockmaker

Even more common than the convinced atheist (who says God definitely does not exist) is the believer in one or another variation of a clockmaker God, the Supreme Being who sets things in motion, like the maker of a good Swiss watch, and leaves us to our own fate.

You may remember the famous book by Harold S. Kushner, *When Bad Things Happen to Good People*. It is loaded with pearls of wisdom. Its greatest merit, I think, is the brutal honesty and humanity with which Rabbi Kushner tells the personal story of dealing with the rare sickness and premature death of his teenage son.

But Rabbi Kushner, by his own admission, comes up with some rather unorthodox conclusions: "God does not want you to be sick or crippled. God didn't make you have this problem, he doesn't want you to go on having it, but he can't make it go away. That is something too hard even for God."

Later he concludes, "I can worship a God who hates suffering but cannot eliminate it, more easily than I can worship a God who chooses to make children suffer and die, for whatever exalted reason."

In other words, God is not strong enough to take away our suffering. The clockmaker God is "out there" but is not really able to affect our reality. He looks down on the world from a distance and can't do anything about our problems or, even worse, doesn't really care.

God the Clockmaker is almost a mythic character. He is the concept we employ to live good lives, or to get others to be good—the "opium of the people," as Karl Marx would put it. What the Bible says is only symbolic, a collection of fairy tales told to children and, strangely, believed even by adults to explain why we should be good. God the Clockmaker is not much more. Religion exists to ensure that society runs efficiently; it allows us to pretend there is meaning, purpose, and long-term consequences to our decisions.

For many who view God as the Clockmaker, suffering is an inevitable reality in life. We should avoid what we can and just put up with the rest.

Much of my research and investigation in the news world brings me face-to-face with grave statistics regarding poverty, disease, corruption, and violence. These figures seem to back up the clock-work and mythic God and one of the more common concepts of God among the television anchors, correspondents, and producers with whom I've worked. The wise Creator has capped his quill pen, they would say, and allowed us essentially to write our own demise. If the world is to be saved, it's up to us, because God isn't about to intervene.

God of the Buffet

A freshman at Brown University once told me of a conversation she had with her roommate the day they met. "Oh that's nice," her friend said. "You believe in God. Well *my* God is like this . . ." And on the friend continued, describing the characteristics of her God of the Buffet.

C. S. Lewis summarizes this attitude in *The Screwtape Letters,* when the experienced devil character, counseling his younger co-hort, boasts of how they have made men confuse the meanings of the word *my,* such that we now say "my God" in the same way we would say "my boots" or "my stereo."

We are accustomed to having our life choices personalized. From computer settings to condiments on our Subway sandwich, everything is made to order. As we go through a buffet line we pick what we want: a salad, a little pasta, roast beef, some potatoes, another veggie, and then some fresh fruit and a little cheesecake to top it off. Likewise we pick out our beliefs. We take Buddhist meditation, Hindu mysticism, the Jesus figure of love and forgive-ness, a touch of New Age—but, please, hold back the morality.

An offshoot of this depiction of the divine is the New Age idea of an all-pervasive energy, force, or cosmic consciousness. It too subordinates God to our whims. We all have the same source and are part of one universal substance: the world is God, I am God, and God is everything. Our interior rhythm and the rhythm of nature are the ways to the Infinite Being. God is not someone for me to know; he is something for me to create.

In the New Age mentality, life events—including suffering— can be attributed to karma. Suffering is in part a result of one's own bad actions. The cosmos is coming back to charge us a toll. It is all part of the ever-rotating wheel of energy that keeps life in balance.

The "God of the Buffet" mentality is at the heart of many of the new religious fads like Kabbalah, Scientology, and New Age beliefs. These fads focus on one or several attractive qualities of God or creation—his healing power, omnipresence, creative intelligence, and so forth—and build a philosophy or religion around these qualities.

In the end, God of the Buffet boils down to intellectual and religious relativism. This mentality holds that truth is subjective, and so each of us can choose his religion at will, all religions being equally valid. Instead of acknowledging that God is perfect, adherents of God of the Buffet see him as mutable. He is employed as a motivating, comforting, or disciplinary force when it's convenient. He vanishes when we no longer believe.

God the Cop

He's the cop just waiting to catch me speeding. If I'm not perfect, he's against me, and eventually he'll catch me. He is the remnants of the wrathful God of fire and brimstone. When bad things happen, it's because he is mad and punishing the world. Tsunamis, hurricanes, earthquakes, broken relationships—God is the cause of our suffering.

When we see God as a cop, we subordinate his attributes of love and forgiveness to images of a vengeful judge—based primarily on false interpretations of Old Testament accounts. So God is not a father. He is not a mother. He is just an old man ticked off by so much sin. We fear that even minor infractions may stir him to strike back, to send a lightening bolt hurling from the heavens.

Catholics with a little bit of religious training, but not enough, are the most likely victims of this vision of God. If you are taught that you can't do something because that's just the way it is, then for you God will always be the bad guy who is impossible to please. Some Protestants tend to go to the other extreme: Yes, God is a cop, but because I am saved, he's always going to let me off the hook. He's a cop who has already done the jail time for me. I can pretty much do whatever I want . . . until my actions start to make me doubt whether I was really saved in the first place.

God as Life Insurance

The Life Insurance God is icing on the cake. During our youth, we don't throw him out altogether. After all, we appreciate the direction of a values-oriented lifestyle. A sense of morality allows us to feel good when we do good. Morals offer a basic guide to interaction with people and generally yield a positive outlook on relationships and life. But being religious will be for later in life, when we've tried everything else and still look for meaning.

In other words, we don't need God now, and he doesn't seem to mind. We're saving him for later. God and faith require too much time and energy. We want to spend the prime of our lives on other things. Not getting too involved also keeps us in the bliss of ignorance. We prefer to live without the guilty conscience that we assume will inevitably accompany the pursuit of religious truth.

I used to work in college campus ministry. One day a young man named Nick, whom I knew very well, came to talk to me. He was an exceptional guy trying to live his faith in the midst of an aggressively anti-Christian environment, as seen in the secular agenda in the classroom and the hedonistic social life on campus. He told me about a girl he was interested in dating and his concern about their compatibility, based on a conversation they had had the night before on one of their early dates. Nick had asked her whether she was religious. She responded by saying that she was spiritual but not religious. Nick had heard this line before and didn't like it much, but now he really wasn't sure what to make of it.

Nick and I talked about what being spiritual and religious really mean. I explained that every human being is spiritual by definition. It's not something special that we do or choose to be. Unlike animals, we are naturally open to the transcendent. We look for love. We try to prolong our lives. We want to know. All of these are indications of our spiritual nature. Spirituality, then, is God's gift to every human being, not any act of virtue on our part.

Religion, on the other hand, from a sociological point of view, is man's response to that gift of spirituality. He hears God's call to his soul and responds in prayer, music, admiring nature, gathering in church, receiving the sacraments, and reading sacred texts, among other things. These are all expressions of our spirituality and efforts to cultivate our relationship with God.

To say, then, "I am spiritual, but not religious," as Nick's friend did, may sound good, but it is really an affirmation that one has chosen not to do anything about one's spirituality. It is saying, *God gave me a gift and I'm not going to use it.*

Now, I also told Nick not to jump to any conclusions about what his girlfriend actually meant, and certainly not about their compatibility. I told him her response most likely reflected what she'd heard on television, seen in the movies, and read in textbooks. It is generally accepted as cool to be spiritual (acknowledging vague sentiments of openness to the presence of a higher power) but as very uncool, and awfully boring, to be religious.

God as Life Insurance, in whatever form he takes, is an impersonal God who remains aloof to our lives and whom we can subject to our own whims, and especially to our own timetable.

The kind of God I have described in these categories is a capricious, weak being at best. If these misconceptions have seeped into your understanding of God, it's perfectly understandable that he's not the kind of God you would turn to for a solution to senseless suffering.

I invite you now to compare these *misconceptions* about God to God himself—who he has revealed himself to be.

Questions for Personal
Reflection or Discussion

➤ How do I conceive God? How would I characterize my relationship with God?

➤ Does my perception of God change in difficult moments?

4

In God We Trust?

*In times past, God spoke in partial and various
ways to our ancestors through the prophets; in these
last days, he spoke to us through a son.*

—HEBREWS 1:1–2

In every civilization people have worshiped God. In awe of
nature, the ancients depicted his creative intelligence in art
and literature, and their mythological figures expressed in
anthropomorphic terms their imagined qualities of the divine—
powerful, vengeful, jealous, and just.

All of this was an expression of man's longing to know God and
communicate with him. But God always seemed distant.

Then B.C. became A.D.

The Christian God is fully revealed in the person of Jesus Christ—
God who knows our deep suffering, physical and spiritual, and came
to earth to make things right, to invite us to be with him forever in
eternity, where every tear will be wiped away.

Humanity rejected God through the original sin of Adam and
Eve, just as we do every time we commit sin. Humans preferred

to "play god" rather than submit themselves to his perfect plan for them. Here man separated himself irreparably from God, and the original harmony in creation, where God was allowed to be God, was lost. Humanity told God to take a hike, and in a certain sense, he did.

But instead of going away forever and abandoning us to the tragic consequences of our own pride, God offered himself in the person of Jesus as a ransom to make things right again. He took our sins upon his back. He reversed the distorted order and prepared a perfect home for us in heaven.

What a far cry Jesus is from a vending machine, clockmaker, cop, buffet, or life insurance! He enters our lives in every way, or, as Scripture says, he became one of us in all things but sin. He is on the side of the one who suffers and is dedicated to bringing good out of evil in every instance.

The Trust Factor

Total trust in God in the face of suffering depends in part upon the vision we have of him, upon how we answer the penetrating question Jesus directed to his apostles: "Who do you say that I am?" (Matt. 16:15).

FROM MY IN-BOX

> I believe he was a great man, an incredible moral teacher, but I don't necessarily think Jesus was God.
>
> —*Dave*

Do you have any friends who think like this? They respect the Bible as a book of inspirational quotes—perfect for a calendar with a tear-away page for each day of the year.

But as long as that's the vision we have of Jesus, he's never going to contribute anything to making sense of our lives and our world of pain. Nonbelieving or nominally Christian politicians and other public figures are especially good at reducing Jesus to inspirational quotes.

People who take this secularized approach to Jesus are off base for at least one of two reasons. Either they believe Jesus never made any astounding assertions about himself, as though he were a moralist or a philanthropist but no more, or they have not contemplated what his claims and actions mean for the world today, especially for those who call themselves Christians.

Religious faith is not blind. It is not irrational. It is about trusting and loving someone we have come to know. If you haven't come to know Jesus personally and as a providential God—one who is on our side—it is irrational to put your trust in him.

That's why those who believe in an all-powerful God, but who don't believe in his willingness to use his power, understandably blame him for their present suffering. They don't consider him trustworthy.

FROM MY IN-BOX

> Praying, asking God for things, and thanking him is nice because it makes us feel good. And that's why I do it. But if I were to be honest, my only prayer would be one of complaint. Who does this God think he is that he can sit up there on his holy throne while we go through hell on earth. He is the one who supposedly put us here. If he did, and now he abandons us, well, he's got nothing to say to me.
>
> —Jim

But has God abandoned us?

Jesus' life and death are God sharing in my suffering out of love for me. They are the ultimate sign of God's *personal* and *providential* nature. A personal God is one with whom we can enter into a relationship. A providential God is one who intervenes in our lives to bring us to full happiness, here on earth and in heaven. Jesus himself is the greatest intervention of the divine in our lives that we could ever ask for. He does more than give good things; he gives himself for our redemption.

Many Catholics and followers of mainline Protestant traditions are turned off by Evangelicals who say things like "Unless you accept Jesus Christ as your personal Lord and Savior, you will not be saved." Evangelicals talk about "the moment of my conversion" or "the day I became a Christian." They are scandalized when Catholics say they don't remember when, if ever, they first "accepted Jesus into their lives." A typical Catholic, even a very fervent one, might say he's been Christian from as far back as he remembers. He would consider a public "acceptance of Jesus" to be redundant. He knows he believes in his heart and, in the best of cases, also confirms this through his words and actions.

But I think Catholics, Orthodox Christians, and traditional Protestants have a lot to learn from Evangelicals in this regard. They remind us that Jesus is not an idea or a concept. He is not a philosophy or a moral code. He is a living person with whom we can form a personal relationship and through whose suffering, death, and Resurrection we have been saved from sin and death and given the opportunity for eternal life and the plenitude of happiness.

In his letter to the Romans, the apostle Paul says, "If you confess with your mouth that Jesus is Lord and believe in your heart that God raised him from the dead, you will be saved" (Rom. 10:9). Although I think there can be various ways to express with our mouths and believe in our hearts, Paul's words cannot be overlooked or explained away.

I bring in this Scripture passage as a way to show how *radical,* so to speak, the Christian faith is, and how starkly it contrasts with the other concepts of God we discussed in the last chapter. Either we accept Jesus as God and savior, or we turn him into something he never claimed to be: just a teacher, moral guide, or social reformer.

What Did He Say About Himself?

A levelheaded perusal of Scripture—and other early Christian documents—suffices to reveal how Jesus differed from the prophets, teachers, and gurus of his day and ours. Nobody can say Jesus was just a good man. Why? Because he claimed to be divine! How many "good guys" do that?

Jesus couldn't have been clearer in this claim than during the trial before the Sanhedrin:

> *Again the high priest asked him and said to him, "Are you the Messiah, the son of the Blessed One?"*
> *Then Jesus answered, "I am; and 'you will see the Son of Man seated at the right hand of the Power and coming with the clouds of heaven.'"*
> *At that the high priest tore his garments and said, "What further need have we of witnesses?*
> *"You have heard the blasphemy. What do you think?"*
> *They all condemned him as deserving to die.*
> *(Mark 14:61–64)*

In chapter 8 of John's Gospel, Jesus is nearly stoned to death for daring to apply to himself God's ineffable name: "I Am" (John 8:58). In chapters 5 and 10 of the same Gospel, his enemies plot to kill him "because he not only broke the sabbath but he also called God his own father, making himself equal to God" (John 5:18).

The apostles eventually understood the fullness of their master's claims. After the Resurrection, Thomas gets over his doubts when he presses his fingers into Jesus' wounds and exclaims, "My Lord and my God!" (John 20:28).

The early Christian community was just as convinced. They worshiped Jesus as God. One of the earliest witnesses after the apostles is Ignatius of Antioch, who wrote in A.D. 110 in chapter 18 of his *Letter to the Ephesians,* "For our God, Jesus Christ, was conceived by Mary in accord with God's plan: of the seed of David, it is true, but also of the Holy Spirit."

In A.D. 225, Origen, referring to Jesus, wrote the following in the preface to *De Principiis* (*The Fundamental Doctrines*): "Although he was God, he took flesh; and having been made man, he remained what he was: God."

You may be surprised to learn that Napoleon, the general and emperor, wrote this about Jesus the Nazarene:

> *I know men; and I tell you that Jesus Christ is not a man. Superficial minds see a resemblance between Christ and the founders of empires, and the gods of other religions. That resemblance does not exist. . . .*
>
> *Everything in Christ astonishes me. His spirit overawes me, and his will confounds me. Between him and whoever else in the world there is no possible term of comparison. He is truly a being by himself. His ideas and his sentiments, the truth which he announces, his manner of convincing, are not explained either by human organization or by the nature of things.*
>
> *. . . I search in vain in history to find the similar to Jesus Christ, or anything which can approach the gospel. Neither history, nor humanity, nor the ages, nor nature, offer me any-*

thing with which I am able to compare it or to explain it. Here
everything is extraordinary.

What is so remarkable about Jesus that even despots like Napoleon
recognize something totally unique in Jesus, something more than
human?

There are only a few intellectually honest ways of sizing up the
historical Jesus: he was either a liar or a lunatic—and possessed
by the devil—or he was the Son of God. In *Mere Christianity,* the
great English apologist C. S. Lewis put it like this:

> *A man who was merely a man and said the sort of things Jesus*
> *said would not be a great moral teacher. He would either be a*
> *lunatic on a level with a man who says he is a poached egg or*
> *else he would have to be the devil of hell. You must make your*
> *choice. Either this man was, and is, the son of God, or a mad-*
> *man or something worse.*

What he can't be is "just a good guy." "The Father is in me and
I am in the Father" (John 10:38). If he lied about that, he is not
good. If he duped millions of disciples to follow him, even to lay
down their lives for his sake, he certainly was not a good man. If he
deliberately deceived us about his identity, he was a blasphemer
and a deceiver to the greatest degree. Add a little supernatural
power to such wickedness (he walked on water, turned water to
wine, made the deaf hear, made the lame walk, made the dead rise
again), and we could almost call that man a devil.

Of course, there's the other side of the coin. If he's telling the
truth, if he truly is divine, if he entered this world out of love for
us to bring us to freedom and happiness, he deserves our love, our
obedience, and our worship. He deserves the humble submission
of our whole lives.

Why Many Still Think He Was
Just a Good Guy

Not long ago I received an e-mail message from a very bright young man named Robert who by his own admission falls into the "Jesus was a good guy" category. He described himself as someone who values "an academic understanding of the Bible." I have no beef with that. The Bible can be studied from many points of view. The problem is the implicit posture Robert's statement assumes, a posture closed to the recognition of anything miraculous, transcendent, or divinely inspired in the life of Jesus.

Dan Brown's religious thriller *The Da Vinci Code* comes to mind as representative of the mind-set of people like Robert who don't know the real Jesus because they have been taught something else by modern culture. There has always been, and continues to be (perhaps with greater strength now than at any other time in modern history), an effort to revise and deconstruct Christian history, beginning with who Jesus claimed to be. *The Da Vinci Code* is among the most recent attempts.

Among many fables found in Brown's best-selling book is the assertion that early Christians saw Jesus as a good teacher or perhaps an enlightened guru, but not as God:

> *Until that moment in history [*A.D. *325, the First Council of Nicaea], Jesus was viewed by His followers as a mortal prophet . . . a great and powerful man, but a man nonetheless. A mortal. . . . By officially endorsing Jesus as the Son of God, Constantine turned Jesus into a deity.*

Anyone with a vague knowledge of early Christian history reads this and tries not to laugh or turn red with anger. We've already cited writings of Ignatius of Antioch and Origen from the second and third centuries that show the falsity of this assertion. Tatian the Syrian, writing in A.D. 170, gives us another clear example in his "Address to the Greeks": "We are not playing the fool, you Greeks, nor do we talk nonsense, when we report that God was born in the form of a man."

Perhaps the greatest proof of the early Christian community's belief in the divinity of Christ are the estimated one hundred thousand to two hundred thousand men and women of the first centuries of Christianity who preferred death by torture to the denial of their faith. The Roman emperors Decius (249–251) and Diocletian (284—305) persecuted Christians because they refused to worship pagan gods. In the Colosseum, in the Circus Maximus, and on the streets of Rome, Christians uttered the name of Jesus as they went to their deaths.

I bring up *The Da Vinci Code* to show how the truth about the Christian God can be easily distorted and how this distortion affects our ability to trust in him for answers. On almost every plane ride that I took during a six-month period, the first question from the passenger next to me was "Father, did you read *The Da Vinci Code?*'" I would always respond with an answer and then a question: "Yes. What did you think?" Surprisingly, not a few people think Dan Brown is more than a great storyteller. They consider him a stellar historian and theologian—a man whose assertions about Jesus are worthy of trust.

In the lead-up to the release of the film version of *The Da Vinci Code,* I spoke often on television and radio about the controversy. People lambasted me for saying Dan Brown was manipulating historical truth. They said I was being judgmental of his intentions, saying the novel was meant for pure escapism and in no way reflected a personal, cynical take on Christianity.

Given the fact that Brown's claims about the made-up nature of the divinity of Jesus Christ were presented in a book of fiction, I could see their point. So I tried to pay attention whenever Brown spoke off the cuff. In talks and conferences leading up to the release of the film, he made his personal position clear. While calling himself a Christian, he regularly put into doubt the most fundamental elements of Christianity's creed.

At a talk in New Hampshire on April 23, 2006, in response to a question about the many books and pamphlets aimed at "decoding" or "debunking" the historic, artistic, and theological claims of his book, he responded, "Those authors and I obviously disagree."

Unfortunately, Dan Brown was capable of passing fiction for fact (and of selling many books) because Christians don't know their faith—what and why they believe. That's not Mr. Brown's fault, but he surely took advantage of it!

Where Do We Go from Here?

This was a simple and very partial review of who Jesus said he was and who Christians have believed him to be for more than two thousand years, despite constant attempts to distort the historic truth. But religious belief is not a simple assent of the intellect to historic fact. It's more than that. Faith is a gift, a grace, a blessing. It is a supernatural bridge between God and man.

Our faith in God is analogous to human love. Anyone who has ever fallen in love knows there is an element of mystery that overtakes you. You can say why you like someone, what attributes about them are attractive to you, but none of that envelops all that is going on in the heart. Normal people don't fall in love with someone's Internet résumé or curriculum vitae. It's the personal connection that does it. It's a meeting of the hearts.

Similarly, reminders about who the Christian God is and what he taught, such as those I have presented here, can prepare the soul to make an act of faith. But they are not enough. God proposes; he doesn't impose. He doesn't give scientific proof of his divinity. He doesn't make us believe with overwhelming, foolproof evidence.

In order to have faith in Jesus, we have to know Jesus—not know of him, or about him, but know *him*.

That blessing doesn't happen on its own. God usually works first through our minds and then the heart. In the following chapter, I will focus on the heart. I will try to explain in simple words how the contemplation of the suffering, death, and Resurrection of Jesus has moved my heart and will, and the heart and will of billions of others, to love him and to trust him, even in the midst of high winds and choppy seas.

Questions for Personal Reflection or Discussion

➤ Do I really trust in God? If not, why not?

➤ Do I have a personal, intimate, and loving relationship with God, as with a close friend?

5

Revealed in Suffering

*But he was pierced for our offenses, crushed
for our sins. Upon him was the chastisement that makes
us whole, by his stripes we were healed.*

— ISAIAH 53:5

I t was partly sunny outside, but the mood on the set was gray.
The filming had been longer, more arduous, and more expensive than the producers had planned, and, worst of all, the
media was catching on that something big—and mysteriously controversial—was playing out at the old and famed Cinecittà movie
studios on the outskirts of Rome.

I stood behind the cameras on the dusty set. Mel Gibson was
absorbed in the images appearing on the director's monitor. He
wanted another take. "Jim, come on down," he called. The makeup
artist jumped at the opportunity to do her thing as the Jesus figure
walked away from Pontius Pilot and down the long, stone steps
of the praetorium, his hands and feet still fettered in heavy iron

shackles. She wanted to dab his swollen eye, but from the sight of things, she was moved more out of genuine pity for Jesus than from any need to make Jim Caviezel look right. Surreal.

It was the making of *The Passion of the Christ*. We knew that this scene, in particular, was crucial to telling the full Gospel story. The pressure was on. Barabbas, the wild-eyed bandit, was playing his part with perfection. He was the antithesis of the innocent man; he was guilty and unrepentant and repulsive on the inside and out. And Pilot, in all his hubris, asks the crowd which of the two, Jesus or Barabbas, they would prefer to be set free.

It was their choice, and ours. Would they favor incarnate evil over incarnate goodness?

Now, had their task been only to determine the guilt or innocence of a lone man accused of blasphemy, of calling God his father, of claiming unjustly to be the Son of God, we could almost pardon a guilty sentence. Sometimes we just get things wrong. But with Barabbas on the scene, things were different; the choice should have been clear, if justice were their cause. His bushy hair and torn clothes meshed perfectly with his loud cries of rebellion. His whole persona pointed a mocking finger at Jesus. The rejection of the crowd was not only about guilt or innocence; it was about getting rid of Jesus the man, the one who challenged them with truth.

When Jim Caviezel stepped behind the cameras and into the director's den, where I now stood, he asked me a question: "What would Jesus have been thinking in this moment? What was going through his mind and heart?" Jim, I think, knew that this was the climax of human history. It was the moment when the crowd, representing all of us sinners, had a chance to give the thumbs-up or thumbs-down to God made man. We could have, in one simple move, overturned Adam and Eve's rejection of God. We could have accepted his forgiveness and allowed him to save us some other way—a bloodless way, with neither cross nor nails. Not to happen. Jim's character knew what the choice would be.

As Jim and I contemplated together the immensity of the moment, the overwhelming stakes at play, and tried to conjure up matching emotions, I looked up and saw Barabbas. He had stayed put when Jim came down the stairs, and he even stayed in character—a slimy, nasty, shameless man who, to my surprise, looked, in that moment, a lot like I felt! "Jim, forget the grandeur of the moment; don't think about a lost humanity. Look at that man," I said. "He looks like us. He's a sinner, and his sin has made him black inside. Darkness has overtaken him. He's in such slavery, he doesn't even know what a savior looks like when he's staring him in the face. What would Jesus be thinking, Jim? He would be thinking about Barabbas, how to bring him back, how to save this one lost sheep." Jim nodded but stayed silent. It's the way God always works, person to person, one-on-one. Jesus didn't go to the cross to save a faceless humanity; he went for you, and he went for me.

Jim exchanged some words with Mel, clutched his own miniature cross hanging from his neck, and shuffled back up the praetorium steps. As he approached the stand, cameras still on hold, Barabbas mumbled a few ironic taunts to make sure Jim knew he was still very much in character. The guy was mean.

Now the cameras rolled. While the crowds continued to ask for Barabbas's release and to yell "Crucify him, crucify him!" to Pilot in reference to Jesus, Jim took his attention for just a moment away from the jeering masses. He moved his weary head ever so slightly and caught the eye of the one lost sheep whom God, his Father, had permitted to be closest by his side. Barabbas was now released, and he was making his own way down the stairs. No shackles. As he slithered away, he felt Jim's look. He turned. For a very long second, their eyes met. The superficial and noisy Barabbas fell deeply silent. Something happened. Jim communicated, on that one take, and without a single word, the loving heart of the Good Shepherd, the reason for the Incarnation of baby Jesus, the power of the cross, and, yes, the ultimate answer to our suffering. His penetrating look said it all: "I know you, and I am with you, my friend, my child, and I love you so much I want nothing more than to suffer and die in your place so you can be truly free." He wanted to say the same to each of us, each member of the jeering crowd.

Now, that was just a movie. But the good news is that it wasn't fiction. It's a movie about a real event, a real God, real love, and real redemption. The actor who played Barabbas, Pedro Sarubbi, has no doubts about this. He wrote the following personal testimony about how God used that staged meeting of his eyes with Jim's to introduce him to the living Jesus, who means exactly what Jim's look portrayed.

Unfortunately, as I gradually became used to the routine of my profession, I lost contact with the research and the quality of life, and became more and more cynical and superficial. Mel Gibson saw me in the film *Captain Corelli's Mandolin* and offered me the part of Barabbas in the film *The Passion*. I was concerned about how big a part I would have, how much they would pay me, and how much publicity it would bring me. I was unhappy to find that Barabbas had nothing to say, something really humiliating for actors of a certain standing. At the end of the screen tests, I went to Mel Gibson and told him I was enthusiastic to work with him, but couldn't accept a non-speaking part. He took me to one side in a fatherly way and explained that this will be a beautiful and very important film and that my dumb Barabbas will be more important for me and for the film than any other speaking role in an ordinary film. "You will use the power of your look, like all the actors in this film!" he told me. We did the filming and I went on complaining. During the third week of filming, when I came down the first stairway of the Sanhedrin, my eyes met the eyes of the actor Jim Caviezel, and it was like an electric shock, a great emotion came over me, and I carried that wonder with me and my life began to change. I have the feeling that something really happened and that look was there, but it was really between Pedro and Christ. It was something enormous and it sent me into complete confusion. Why did it happen? This question keeps coming back to me.

In the last chapter I hope we were able to remove a few of the intellectual barriers that keep us from trusting in God's love and power, but our question still has not been answered. *Why doesn't God do anything to stop my pain?*

Here we are assuming that suffering is bad, that there is something essentially wrong with it. We are taking for granted that the world would be better if all were bliss. If this is the way we think . . . we're on the right track. We are thinking like God. Health is better than sickness. Love is better than hate.

But obedience is also better than disobedience, and we chose the latter: Adam and Eve traded the Garden of Eden for this valley of tears. And I myself trade it every time I choose selfishness over love.

In God's divine wisdom, he knew how to bring a "greater good" even out of our disobedience. It is the Incarnation, suffering, death, and Resurrection of Jesus Christ. He made sweet the tears of our earthly valley. Jesus turns original sin and all of our personal sin—the causes of evil and all suffering—upside down. By taking upon himself the sin of the world and enduring every form of suffering, he opens for us the door to eternal life . . . the door we shut and locked with the abuse of our free will.

A Man like Us

The "mere" fact of the Incarnation already provides a stunning response to the seeming absurdity of human suffering. God sent his only begotten son to span the chasm between God and man. It was an abyss no human being could have muscled his way across. That's what the baby in the manger tells us every Christmas. "I came to you! I'm Emmanuel, God is with you!"

But the mystery of the Incarnation didn't end on Christmas morning. For thirty silent years in Nazareth, Jesus shared everything we suffer. Jesus was true God, yes. But he was also true man. With a human body and human soul, Christ wasn't immune to any human pain—physical or spiritual, corporal or moral. As a man, he must have gotten blisters and stomachaches, splinters and hangnails. As a man, he knew heartache. The Almighty chose to assume our impotence.

He even submitted himself to the temptation of sin, just like us, and, unlike us, in every struggle he triumphed (Heb. 4:15). We know what an interior suffering it is to resist the temptation to sin. Sin always presents itself in camouflage, selling itself as attractive, even irresistible. The quick and easy way to end the suffering is to give in to the temptation and gratify disordered passions. But Jesus never gave in. He never betrayed his Father's love. Jesus was spotless: "Can any of you charge me with sin?" (John 8:46).

Those little details help me marvel over God's decision to take on our human weakness. The King of kings grew up in poverty. He knew what it was like to be ridiculed and laughed at. His neighbors thought nothing of him, even as they watched his miracles. They scoffed, "Is he not the carpenter?" (Mark 6:3).

Solidarity in suffering, Jesus suffering with us, is already a great consolation, an enduring sign of his goodness and love. He longed to be with us always. Love is like that. The lover says, "I'll always be there—in sickness and in health, for richer or for poorer." And that was precisely Jesus' last word to humanity. As he ascended into heaven, he didn't say good-bye; he said, "And behold, I am with you always, until the end of the age" (Matt. 28:20).

For me, and I think for most of us, the most difficult scene of *The Passion* to watch is the scourging. And we saw only the toned-down version. Mel originally planned for the scene to be even more graphic, something representative of the estimated one hundred lashings depicted on the Shroud of Turin. I remember being on the set during the scourging scene. It was eerie. Nobody talked.

"I want to push them over the edge," Mel said. Some critics came down hard on him for all the violence. More than one critic said, "There's something wrong with a movie about Jesus Christ being rated R." Mel's response hit the nail on the head: "There's something wrong with crucifying the Son of God."

No one in the history of the world knew more excruciating (from the Latin *ex-cruciatus,* "out of the cross") pain than the Savior nailed to the cross: "Come, all you who pass by the way, look and see whether there is any suffering like my suffering"(Lam. 1:12).

We need smart eyes to see why Jesus' suffering was like nobody else's.

When Jesus was hanging on the cross, he was sustaining the existence of the nails in his hands and feet and the thorns piercing his forehead. He empowered the sinners that turned against him in fury. He gave them existence and free will, and he sustained these gifts, even when they were used to destroy him. Without his love and power, there is no human freedom. There is no gift to us.

And without his gift, there is no passion for him to suffer. And yet, he keeps giving.

The crown of thorns, the scourging, the nails in his hands and feet—these were just the beginning. A 125-pound cross is heavy, but he was bearing another cross—an invisible one. The visible one weighing down on his shoulders symbolizes the invisible one weighing down on his spirit. Jesus' deepest suffering was emotional and spiritual, much like ours.

Why So Much Sorrow?

The night before Jesus' crucifixion, he went off with his disciples to the Garden of Gethsemane to pray. Judas, the betrayer, knew the place well and eventually led the guards there to arrest him. But first Jesus would endure heart-wrenching and body-busting anguish. The Scriptures say he sweat "drops of blood," a phenomenon doctors say can be caused by extreme emotional grief.

It is the contemplation of this Gospel scene that has most helped me come to love Jesus and work to conform my life to his. It has also been the greatest consolation to me in moments of personal failure and sadness.

I'll try to explain why. I always assumed Jesus suffered in Gethsemane primarily out of fear of his pending crucifixion. The man on death row doesn't sleep the night before his execution. The mere thought of thorns in the head, lashes on the back, and nails in the hands and feet would be enough to break the psyche.

Jesus certainly experienced fear, just like us, but the agony in the Garden was about something else. "I am sorrowful, even to death," Jesus said to Peter, James, and John.

A sorrowful soul is one besieged by sadness, grief, or guilt. The emotions are constant. They throb. We feel them bubbling within us.

In Jesus' case, they bubbled over: "Look and see whether there is any suffering like my suffering, which has been dealt me" (Lam. 1:12).

It wasn't just quantity. The intensity had to do with the source of his sorrow. According to this passage from the book of Lamentations, Jesus' sorrow was heaped upon him from without. In other words, he was suffering what we should suffer. He was living our grief. He was carrying our sorrow.

> *Yet it was our infirmities that he bore, our sufferings that*
> *he endured,*
> *While we thought of him as stricken, as one smitten by*
> *God and afflicted.*
> *But he was pierced for our offenses, crushed for our sins.*
> *(Isa. 53:4–5)*

Crushed for our sins!? Have you ever been crushed by sin? I have. It's the feeling we get when we have harmed someone we love. It is the knot in our stomach and the self-directed anger that eats away at our mind. Think for a moment of your biggest sin, what most damaged your relationship to God and others. It doesn't have to look ugly to be ugly. It's the things we never should have said, the visits to friends and family we should have made, the lying, backbiting, cheating, gossip, and infidelities to our vows.

It was for this and these that Jesus felt sorrow. But his sorrow wasn't pity. "Oh, poor people, poor sinners who didn't know how to appreciate my love for them." No way. Jesus felt the sorrow for our sin as if the sin were his own. That's what taking upon our sin meant, and that's why he was crushed: "For our sake he made him to be sin who did not know sin, so that we might become the righteousness of God in him"(2 Cor. 5:21).

It helps me to picture Jesus going to the Father and saying that he, Jesus, was the guilty one: "Father, Father, I am sorry. I did this and this and this. I also did that . . . and yes, that, too." There were no excuses. The finger he should have pointed at us he pointed at himself. The sinless one became sin itself. Imagine the weight. Jesus at this moment couldn't care less about thorns, nails, and crosses. He is feeling the real cross. It is the burden of humanity's rejection of the love of God, year after year and in every society on the face of the earth: "We had all gone astray like sheep, each following his own way; But the Lord laid upon him the guilt of us all" (Isa. 53:6).

That's a kind of man I'd like to die for. He did for me.

There is a second moment in the passion of Jesus that helps me in a special way to know and love him more. It is at the very end of his ordeal. He is nearly breathing his last.

It is the opening line of Psalm 22: *"Eli, Eli, lama sabachtani."* ("My God, my God, why have you abandoned me?")

The Psalm continues, and maybe Jesus did, too: "Why so far from my call for help, from my cries of anguish? My God, I call by day, but you do not answer; by night, but I have no relief" (Ps. 22:2–3).

It may seem borderline sacrilegious, but these words of the Psalmist, which Jesus chose to repeat, sound like those of a man who is deeply depressed. Anyone who has suffered depression would say he would prefer a million times over to suffer physical pain than to be caught in his world of despair, surrounded by many and forsaken by all.

Jesus suffered this, too. He suffered with your depression. He went to the very end of the rope. He went where we are ashamed to be. But, different than us, in his human despair he never lost spiritual hope. Here's how we know.

The chronology of events during Jesus' last moments varies in the four Gospels. But only Luke gives us a definitive statement of what Jesus' very last words were. Remember, Jesus had just expressed to the whole world his feelings of abandonment. God, his Father, the one who sent him to earth to reunite mankind to himself, seemed in these moments to be far, far away. But for Jesus there was a difference between feelings and facts. God seemed far away. He seemed indifferent to his suffering, as if he were in hiding.

But Jesus had absolute certainty God was near. So again he cried out, now using very different words: "Into your hands I commend my spirit."

Into whose hands? Yes, into the hands of the one who had abandoned him.

What Difference Did It Make?

I will never forget one woman's comment to me after seeing *The Passion*. With sad eyes she slowly said, almost whispering, "After all he suffered, after all he went through for us, what difference did it make? Look at all the hatred, anger, and violence."

I don't recall now what I said to her in the moment, but I have never forgotten the question. Yes, his passion opened the door of paradise, but look at us now!

Rivaling the mystery of the Trinity is the mystery of free will. God proposes, but he never imposes. Sometimes I wish he would.

If our lives are unchanged, we simply have not let the force of love penetrate our hearts. We have watched but not seen. Christ's sacrifice was perfect. It was redemptive "once for all" (Heb. 7:27). All the transforming power remains in his cross, fully charged, surging like a high-voltage generator. We need but plug ourselves in.

But where there's high voltage, we know there's always a warning. What will happen if I allow him to enter my life? We read that warning and flee out of fear. Change is daunting. We don't plug in because we prefer our path. "I'm a nice guy." "I don't hurt anybody." "I'm good enough."

But God isn't content with making us "good enough" because that wouldn't be authentic love. He finds ways of calling out to us even when we don't want to hear. When we aren't open to his invitations, he makes use of other methods. "God whispers in our pleasures but shouts in our pains. Pain is His megaphone to rouse a dulled world," wrote C. S. Lewis in *The Problem of Pain*.

That's what we're about to see in greater detail: how God brings good out of evil, even the evil of our sinfulness that nailed Jesus to a cross, and the consequences of that evil, including my present world of pain and its meaninglessness.

Questions for Personal Reflection or Discussion

➤ What does Christ's suffering mean to me? Does it move me? Does it make me want to love him in return?

➤ How can I apply the message of Christ's suffering to my own life?

6

In Court

Do not be conquered by evil but conquer evil with good.

—ROMANS 12:21

I t's easy for Christians to look down in scorn on the various modern concepts of the divine. We can see them as facile attempts to replace the true Christian God with a feel-good imposter of humanity's own liking and making.

But we would be dishonest to overlook the compelling reasons for which so many people prefer one or another form of what we might consider "diet spirituality," the easy road. The greatest charge against the Christian God is our world of hurt—the suffering of the innocent—and that is nothing to frown at.

Even if our own set of sufferings is minor, we are rightly scandalized when we glance over our shoulders at the "refuse" of the world—the homeless, drug addicts, the abused, and the desperately poor. We struggle to come to grips with the idea of one of God's creatures knowing *only* pain, hatred, disdain, or some other evil.

But there's something else that makes this suffering even worse. It's the interior conflict between suffering and wanting to be free. In the middle of this confusion and dissatisfaction we long for the fullness of happiness. That means we live for something we can't seem to get. This is the problem with pain and evil. It seems God made us to suffer. If God can stop suffering and chooses not to, it would seem that humanity is the greatest cosmic tease of all time.

My quest for sense in suffering is also personal. It's hard to measure how much I've really suffered. On a scale from one to ten, ten being what Jesus suffered and five being any one of the genocides of the last century, my pain wouldn't even register. But if I were to stop and think about what I've seen—injustices committed both by me and against me, and above all against people whom I love—I would have plenty of reason to cry. If I were to add up all of the good times—the joyful family reunions, the good meals, the great baseball, football, and soccer games, and even more spiritual things like friendships, family, commitment, and intimate moments of prayer—I would still have a hard time saying that these outweigh, on a human level, the past and future suffering I will likely bear.

If full and uninterrupted happiness is forever and irrevocably out of reach, the God who fashioned us is a trickster. If suffering is senseless, man is nature's goof or, as Macbeth put it, "a poor player that struts and frets his hour upon the stage, and then is heard no more." His entire existence is an absurdity, "a tale told by an idiot, full of sound and fury, signifying nothing."

Real-Life Misery

Macbeth had seen real-life misery. We've seen it, too.

In fall 2005 I went to France to cover the street riots of Muslim youth in the Parisian suburbs. You might remember the burning cars. At the height of the chaos, the vandals—teenage kids—were setting ablaze four hundred cars a night with Molotov cocktails. The stark and scary images ruled the airwaves.

As the days went on, the revelers became increasingly bold. Soon French officials were reporting copycat vandalism and other violence in every major city within their borders. Some of the violence even spilled over into Germany.

Because the youth were predominantly Muslim, the fear was that the unrest was indicative of a budding Islamic jihad in the heart of Europe. Like it or not, that's the way we think now.

I went into the neighborhoods where the violence started, housing projects about an hour outside of Paris. I talked to the kids, with and without the cameras rolling. I've seen much worse poverty in Latin America, but never have I seen so much despair. These were neighborhoods into which the police had openly declared they wouldn't enter out of fear of reprisal attacks. These were second-generation immigrant adolescents and young adults who had been disenfranchised from French society. More than 35 percent of Muslim and African youth in these parts between the ages of fifteen and twenty-four are unemployed.

More tragic even than the youths' predicament of poverty and violence was the despair among the adults. They knew that their kids were rioting out of anger and desperation, and they knew that the causes would not go away. At one point I did what in the news world is called a "man on the street" interview to get the feel for what ordinary folk were saying. We didn't air it because the translation was choppy, but it went something like this:

Father J: Do you know the kids who are rioting?

Woman: Yes, they live here.

Father J: You know them personally?

Woman: Yes, they are our kids, our young people.

Father J:	Are you concerned?
Woman:	Concerned? Yes, things are bad. They have no work. They have no future. We already know that. Things will never change.
Father J:	And what are you going to do?
Woman:	There's nothing to do. That's life.

This good woman was probably right. There was not much she alone could do about the social strife in her adoptive nation. Her kids would probably end up much like her.

But "That's life?"

I can't say for sure what she meant, but her statement is reflective of an attitude that forms when someone is suffering without meaning and without the slimmest ray of light in the darkness: "Luckily, life is short."

But think for a minute about this woman's situation. She found no joy in life, no sense in life, and she saw absolutely no hope for her kids. Sometimes people in her situation make their lives shorter than they should be, and I can hardly blame them. If "that's life," as she says, either God isn't the all-loving and all-powerful being we think he is, or he has some explaining to do.

Here's another look into the grizzly reality of despair:

FROM MY IN-BOX

I am angry at God for allowing me to suffer for nine years from chronic depression. I've been on every medication; right now I am on the highest dose of the strongest antidepressant and it's useless. God gave me three beautiful healthy children yet a mind incapable of enjoying them. He gave me a loyal, faithful, loving husband, yet not the capacity to stay in love with him (we are getting divorced). I am smart and attractive and a talented writer but none of these things matter because I am dead inside. I've prayed for nine years for God to spare me this pain. He doesn't help. I almost succeeded in killing myself three years ago. My children don't have a functional mother. I am angry at God for playing favorites, for allowing suffering to go on for too long. I used to be vibrant and full of life. Depression has stolen all that away from me, and God won't do a damn thing.

—Melissa

Melissa puts it so well. For her, reconciling the coexistence of God and so much pain is impossible. I think it's fair to say that Melissa has decided, or fears, that either God is not all-powerful or he's not all-loving.

"BUT CHRISTIANITY SAYS GOD IS ALL-POWERFUL . . ."

In thinking about God's supposed power, I can't fail to bring Rabbi Kushner back into our discussion. Do you remember the two quotations I gave earlier?

> *God does not want you to be sick or crippled. God didn't make you have this problem, he doesn't want you to go on having it, but he can't make it go away. That is something too hard even for God.*
>
> *I can worship a God who hates suffering but cannot eliminate it, more easily than I can worship a God who chooses to make children suffer and die, for whatever exalted reason.*

The rabbi comes to the conclusion that because he has seen children suffer and die, and because he wants to believe in an all-loving God, God must not be all-powerful. Amazingly, the rabbi has no problem with forgiving God's weakness. I can't forgive that! Whoever that good but impotent creature is, he surely isn't God. If we look around at nature, we can only stand in awe of the Creator's power. If he can make birds that chirp and eyes that see, why couldn't he stop my suffering right now if he wanted to? Of course he could. Nor can I accept the hypothesis that the Creator stepped away from his marvelous work and somehow disconnected himself from the source of his might and power. God is his own source of power. If he were to disconnect, he would stop being God, and not even God can do that.

Christianity and other major monotheistic religions have always taught that God is all-powerful. His strength is written about throughout Sacred Scripture—the Old Testament and the New Testament.

> O Lord God, almighty King, all things are in your power,
>   and there is no one to oppose you in your will to save
>   Israel.
> You made heaven and earth and every wonderful thing under
>   the heavens.
> You are Lord of all, and there is no one who can resist you,
>   Lord. (Esth. C:2–4)

> [A son] who sustains all things by his mighty word. (Heb. 1:3)

It would seem God just doesn't want to use his power to stop the hurt. Maybe he's not all-loving!

"BUT CHRISTIANITY SAYS GOD IS ALL-LOVING . . ."

I don't think we need many examples to show Christianity's insistence on God's unconditional love. If love is a good thing and if God is not all-loving, it means God is limited in his goodness. A limited being, however grand that being might be, is not God.

The Old Testament points to God's love in many places: "The Lord is merciful and gracious, slow to anger and abounding in steadfast love" (Ps. 103:8). The New Testament reveals God's love as his attribute par excellence: "God is love" (1 John 4:16).

Part of God's all-loving nature is his allowing us to be fully human. Being human means we are endowed with free will. He respects our capacity to choose, even when our choices have some pretty tragic consequences. If he were to step in and reverse every one of our bad decisions in order to prevent us from suffering, would that be love? Would we really be free? We might be free of suffering, but we wouldn't be free to love and to be loved. God loves us so much he himself is even willing to suffer watching us, his children, suffer.

Our world of hurt was not part of God's original plan, but we have turned that perfect plan on its head. Can we really blame God for liars, cheaters, murderers, and abusers and how they affect us when it is we, not he, who have chosen the hard way?

The massacre of thirty-two students at Virginia Tech University by Cho Seung-Hui triggered a national conversation about what could make a young man like this do such a horrible thing, and who is responsible. I was dismayed to hear the level of dialogue. People were happy to debate school security, gun laws, psychiatric medicine, and immigration policy. Politicians at every level began proposing bills to keep our children safe or safer. Universities rolled out revised programs for freshman-orientation weekend. Police forces outlined new and improved first-response strategies.

Yes, those are all good things. But if you scratched the surface just a little bit, as I tried to do on television and the radio, it became clear everybody knew that none of these proposals would make a significant difference. Practical solutions will never get to the heart of a problem when the problem is the human heart itself. Cho Seung-Hui was a man whose heart and mind had rotted from within. For whatever set of complicated reasons, *he* pulled the trigger, and other people suffered. I don't think we can blame God for that. Free will is a free gift, but its consequences are not cheap.

But let's not let God off the hook so easy. If he is all-loving and all-powerful, why didn't he think of a backup plan, knowing we would choose selfishness over obedience? And besides, what about all the suffering caused by so-called acts of God like tsunamis and earthquakes? We can't blame those on free will, or can we?

The Promise

Believe it or not, I think we can, but only under one condition: if, somehow, God could bring out a greater good—something even better than the good that has been lost—from every case of suffering and evil.

This is the Promise! It is God's response to a world that hurts.

Augustine of Hippo—a fourth-century genius and holy man—put it like this in his *Enchiridion:* "God is so good that he would never *permit* anything evil to occur, unless he were powerful enough to be able to draw good from every instance of evil [emphasis added]." Peter Kreeft, in his book *Making Sense out of Suffering,* said it in a different way: "In a universe created and maintained by a God powerful enough to abolish all suffering at once, loving enough to want only our blessedness, and wise enough to know always what makes for our blessedness, the only reason serious enough to justify God's continued tolerance of suffering is our need for it."

"Our need for it" . . . meaning, what will lead us to our absolute fulfillment as human beings—a much greater good.

Both the Old and New Testaments are testimonies of God's power and design to bring good out of evil. This power and design is, in fact, the beginning, middle, and end of the story of our redemption.

Paul's letter to the Romans gives the most succinct summary of God's Promise: "We know that God works out all things for the good for those who love him" (Rom. 8:28).

On the fulfillment of this Promise hinges the very nature of God, all-loving and all-powerful. From every evil, from every bit of our emotional, spiritual, and physical suffering, he will bring forth for the world and for us—if we let him—something even greater than what we now so badly miss. The history of salvation, including the painful twists and turns of each of our lives, is a narration of this Promise working itself out in time and space. It is the story of God saving man from himself.

God's Promise is a divine covenant with man: "And behold, I am with you always, until the end of the age" (Matt. 28:20).

In the quote from Augustine of Hippo, I italicized the word *permit* because it's necessary to make the distinction between God's "permissive will" and his "active will." Stay with me; it sounds complicated, but it's refreshingly simple. God actively causes good things (life itself, for example), but because he is all good he cannot cause evil. God doesn't drop the boom on anyone. He *permits* evil—either the bad things people inflict on themselves and others or the suffering caused by an imperfect physical world—out of respect for our free will and in order to bring out a greater good.

Look back at Rabbi Kushner's words. He said he couldn't worship "a God who *chooses to make* children suffer and die."(Again, I have added the emphasis.) This is why the distinction I make here is important. I agree with Kushner; I could never worship a God who chooses to make anyone suffer or die. As I will now explain, however, I can worship a God who *permits* tragedy out of respect for our free will and who brings forth, in the short or long term, even greater happiness and goodness than what existed before.

A parent who has lost a child in a tragic accident would surely roll his eyes in disgust at the idea of God bringing forth a "greater good" from his child's death. I want to work our way up, little by little, to see how this principle of the "greater good" may be consistent even with the inconsolable suffering of a parent's tragic loss, perhaps the greatest suffering imaginable. We'll start with natural hints.

Even without recurring to faith—that God will miraculously bring good out of every instance of evil—we can see the principle at work by exercising our minds. We can see how suffering does produce positive effects that would not have existed had we not gone through the trouble.

Think about the following natural hints. (Remember, they are just hints, not proofs.)

From pain comes gain.

It's a little bit like working out at the gym. If we want to get in shape, it's got to hurt. This simple principle, in fact, is written all over nature: the winter preludes the spring and night turns into day; a seed has to fall to the ground and decompose for a flower to bloom; a mother's birth pangs brings forth a newborn baby.

Tony Dungy, the head coach of the Indianapolis Colts football team, has had firsthand experience of why pain is sometimes a very good thing, and not just on the practice field. His youngest son, Jordan, has a rare congenital condition that causes him not to feel pain. On the day before his team's win over the Chicago Bears in Super Bowl XLI, Dungy told the following story to a public gathering.

> "Jordan feels things, but he doesn't get the sensation of
> pain. That sounds like it's good at the beginning, but I

promise you it's not. We've learned a lot about pain in the last five years we've had Jordan. We've learned some hurts are really necessary for kids. Pain is necessary for kids to find out the difference between what's good and what's harmful.

"Cookies are good, but in Jordan's mind, if they're good out on the plate, they're even better in the oven. He will go right in the oven when my wife's not looking, reach in, take the rack out, take the pan out, burn his hands and eat the cookies and burn his tongue and never feel it. He doesn't know that's bad for him. He has no fear of anything, so we constantly have to watch him. We've learned that a lot of times because of that pain, that little temporary pain, you learn what's harmful. You learn to fear the right things. Pain sometimes lets us know we have a condition that needs to be healed."

Yes, from pain comes gain.

Suffering makes us more human.

A person who has suffered deeply and triumphed is now a better person. Precisely because of pain and suffering, his life story is better. He has forged character; he has become more human. Would you confide in someone who has never made a tough decision? Don't you love a person more with whom you have suffered side by side?

In *War and Peace,* Tolstoy put it like this: "If there were no suffering, man would not know his limitations, would not know himself."

Think for a moment of those who avoid suffering at all cost. Our Hollywood celebrities, with all their money and power—how are they doing? They can afford vacation getaways, oceanfront properties, and prescription painkillers. But why are so many of them instead in rehab centers and divorce court? By escaping suffering, they have sacrificed their humanity.

We shine when times are bad.

In times of crisis, the best of human nature comes out. Think of the terrorist attacks of 9/11. Our coming together as a nation, though it lasted only a short time, was beautiful. We would not know our capacity for such unity had we not suffered such pain. This happens in almost all tragedy. The outpouring of charity and generosity—and not just material goods—after natural disasters like the Asian tsunami or Hurricane Katrina is a real good that can't be overlooked.

The ancient philosopher Boethius says it beautifully in *The Consolation of Philosophy*:

> *For this reason a wise man should never complain, whenever he is brought into strife with fortune; just as a brave man cannot properly be disgusted whenever the noise of battle is heard, since for both of them their very difficulty is their opportunity, for the brave man of increasing his glory, for the wise man of confirming and strengthening his wisdom. From this is virtue itself so named, because it is so supported by its strength that it is not overcome by adversity.*

When times are bad, when life hurts, we can shine.

That's Not Enough

But for all of that, when a loved one dies an agonizing and senseless death, natural hints about how God might bring forth a greater good from every instance of evil fall dreadfully short.

Do you remember where you were when the Columbia space shuttle blew to bits on that clear Saturday morning of February 1, 2003? Do you remember the feeling? Seven astronauts had just spent the greatest days of their lives in space, but they never came back to tell their stories. What good could come from that?

On the very day of the accident, NASA associate administrator Bill Readdy, a veteran of two shuttle flights, seemed to grasp a way that good might come from his colleagues' loss: "My promise to the crew and to the crew families is that the investigation that we have just launched will find the cause, we'll fix it and then we'll move on. We can't let their sacrifice be in vain."

His last sentence may not have consoled the grieving families, but his words pointed to something we can all imagine. What if the research and new safety measures put in place by NASA after the explosion were responsible for saving the lives of many other astronauts? Is that not a greater good?

Yes and no—and this is where the natural hints come crashing down. It's good for the ones who have been saved, but it's not so good for the seven on board.

Death—or endless suffering—trumps every natural good we can think of. That's why simplistic calculations of the proportion between good and bad consequences work only to a certain point. When the excruciating suffering is my own or when death is knocking at the door, pure reason may help, but it comes up short.

Still using our reason, but looking now at the supernatural realm, we can discern that through suffering we gain spiritual goods, and these goods have added value.

Spiritual goods.

Coach Dungy is a good example. Learning from his five-year-old son's congenital disease, he saw how pain, on a natural level, brings about some good. But later in the same talk he took the principle quite a bit further. His words can best be understood in the context of his own deep personal suffering. Just one year before this talk, his oldest son, James, at the age of eighteen, died in an apparent suicide. "Sometimes, pain is the only way that will turn us, as kids, back to the Father," he said.

Of course, Coach Dungy is not saying he is glad his son died so he and others could learn from this painful experience and get right with the Heavenly Father. No. But he is saying that even in inexplicable tragedy, God can bring forth *spiritual good,* and he does.

Peter Kreeft seems to have had an insider's read of God's playbook. He inadvertently summed up my own experience in these words, again from *Making Sense out of Suffering:* "Suffering fills the need to continually remind us of the most obvious and evident truth there is, yet the one we are most constantly forgetting in practice: that we are not God."

In *The Problem of Pain,* C. S. Lewis had a similar intuition: "We are not merely imperfect creatures who need to grow; we are rebels who need to lay down our arms"; and again, "God whispers in our pleasures but shouts in our pains. Pain is His megaphone to rouse a dulled world."

Again, in his letter to the Romans, the apostle Paul deals with the role of suffering in the Christian life and encourages us to "rejoice" because of the spiritual goods of the *tempering* of our character and our growth in *supernatural virtue.*

> *Not only that, but we even boast of our afflictions, knowing*
> *that affliction produces endurance,*
> *and endurance, proven character, and proven character,*
> *hope,*
> *and hope does not disappoint, because the love of God has*
> *been poured out into our hearts through the holy Spirit that*
> *has been given to us. (Rom. 5:3–5)*

Some spiritual goods that come out of our suffering are also for others. Do you remember the story of Jesus curing the man born blind in the Pool of Siloam?

> *As he passed by he saw a man blind from birth.*
> *His disciples asked him, "Rabbi, who sinned, this man or his*
>   *parents, that he was born blind?"*
> *Jesus answered, "Neither he nor his parents sinned; it is so*
>   *that the works of God might be made visible through*
>   *him." (John 9:1–3)*

For the last two thousand years people have come to know God's power and love by reading the story of this blind man. What if he had not been born blind? He may never have experienced God's love for him, and you and I would never have contemplated this work of God.

Eternal Goods

But still, this is not enough. If we take all the human goods we have gained from suffering and add them to these spiritual goods, can we really say God has brought forth a "greater good" than the original loss?

Rabbi Kushner and I agree; the answer is: "Not always." As he writes in *When Bad Things Happen to Good People*:

> *I am a more sensitive person, a more effective pastor, a more*
> *sympathetic counselor because of [my son] Aaron's life and*
> *death than I would ever have been without it. And I would*
> *give up all of those gains in a second if I could have my son*
> *back. If I could choose, I would forgo all the spiritual growth*
> *and depth which has come my way because of our experi-*
> *ences, and be what I was fifteen years ago, an average rabbi,*

an indifferent counselor helping some people and unable to
help others, and the father of a bright, happy boy. But I cannot
choose.

A friend of mine put the same point to me in different terms,
wondering how God could possibly bring a greater good out of the
death of the innocent:

> Perhaps a year ago I read in the newspaper of a terrible
> incident in which a fourteen-year-old boy got in his mother's
> car with his three- and four-year-old siblings and took it for
> a ride. The car was back-ended, shoved into another car,
> and in the ensuing flames the three were burned to death.
> Quite surely God could have prevented it.
>
> —*Doug*

Yes, I think God could have prevented the burning of these
three children, and also the death of Rabbi Kushner's son. I also
agree no combination of human and spiritual goods can together
be more valuable than the loss of these innocent lives . . . unless
. . . and here's the clincher . . . unless there is a heaven where
all wrongs are made right and if these untimely tragedies fit into
God's mysterious plan of offering every soul, from all times and
in every corner of the world, the chance to get in, including those
who die and those who mourn their loss.

> *He will wipe every tear from their eyes, and there shall be no*
> *more death or mourning, wailing or pain, for the old order*
> *has passed away. (Rev. 21:4)*

So we don't have a *solution*—at least not a definitive one—to
the problem of suffering unless someday suffering is no more. As

long as we consider our fleeting life on earth our only chance for absolute fulfillment, we will logically always point an accusatory finger at the God of love and power.

FROM MY IN-BOX

> I recall when a tumor was taken from my lung which was surprisingly not cancerous (I had been a smoker). The chap that furnished contact lenses to my office referred to "God saving me." I asked him why he did not save the chap near me in the hospital who had three small children and had never smoked. No response. I cannot believe that God can be a capricious God who picks and chooses as he wishes to intervene in one's life. Please respond to me on this one.
>
> —*Doug [again]*

Doug brings up a chilling question and presents it in a fabulous way. He is honest and, I believe, justified in rejecting the idea of a capricious God subject to quirky whims. We are right to shudder at the thought of a God who loves some and not others, who makes some happy and others forever sad.

But when we bring into the equation of the "greater good" an eternal resting place—heaven—God is no longer necessarily capricious when he permits some to live and others to die, some to laugh and others to cry. If God is most interested in our long-term happiness, and if that eternal reward is made possible by accepting God in our lives, we can imagine, though never understand perfectly, why he might choose to intervene only sometimes. It may be the very best thing for us or for our loved one to suffer for a time. It may be the perfect act of love.

God's ways are often mysterious and inscrutable to our limited human intelligence, but as I hope I have shown, their grandeur doesn't make them irrational.

A big part of the mystery of the relationship between free will and God's plan for us is the role of prayer. When we pray, does anything happen? Or is everything predetermined, either by the laws of nature or by the will of God? Many studies have shown that hospital patients who pray fare better. There are also myriad examples of inexplicable and sudden cures. Doctors don't declare these things miracles, in the strict sense of the word. They simply say they don't have any medical explanation.

The efficacy of prayer to move the heart of God to intervene in our lives—to perform a miracle—cannot be proven. But people who believe in Jesus as the Son of God have good reason to trust in his willingness to give us blessings when we ask for them. God's pedagogy, his divine business plan, has always been to involve human beings in his good work.

Have you ever wondered why it is necessary that a man and woman come together for new life to spring forth? Why couldn't God have made us grow on trees, sprout from the earth, float down from the heavens, or simply appear out of nowhere? And doctors. Why the need for all of those years of study when we believe God is quite capable of healing us each and every time we get sick? On a spiritual level, why does he need the prophets to speak his word? Or why did he depend on human beings to pen the Sacred Scriptures? Could he not have hand-delivered a signed copy? Could he not have made us with an embedded computer chip, an internal Wikipedia Web site with 100 percent reliable information about God and man?

I think the best answer comes from the life of Christ. How did he relate to people? Did he heal them from afar? Did he snap his fingers and make them believe? No. He involved people in their own healing and conversion, and more often than not, he waited for them to ask.

Knowing we would still have doubts about whether God wants us, even now, to ask him for blessings, Jesus left us some crystal-clear reminders that God's pedagogy continues: "Ask and it will be given to you; seek and you will find; knock and the door will be opened to you" (Matt. 7:7); "If you then, who are wicked, know how to give good gifts to your children, how much more will your heavenly Father give good things to those who ask him" (Matt. 7:11).

Good things. This is what God wants to give us when we ask. When we don't get what we want, we naturally assume, if we are humble, that the requested gift may not, in fact, be the best thing for us, at least not at this time.

One Last Question

Even if we can accept suffering as part of God's playbook to bring us to true fulfillment and happiness here on earth and also in heaven, we still wonder why he couldn't work this out some other way.

I think the answer has several parts. The first has to do with the origin of suffering. Was suffering part of God's original plan? We will look at this in more detail in the appendix, where we will confront the mystery of suffering and its relationship to evil.

Second, although God could have snapped his fingers from heaven and redeemed us from far, far away, he preferred to redeem us in an utterly human way. God's suffering with us is as beautiful as it is radical. At times we may prefer a less painful path of God's will, but would we prefer a less human path?

Finally, Scripture points to a "spirituality of suffering." In light of very clear biblical passages and the teaching of many holy men and women, we see how God uses suffering as a privileged path to holiness. When we learn, together with the apostle Paul, to unite our suffering to the suffering of Christ, that suffering takes on supernatural value. In the lives of many saints, suffering has become the favorite companion on the journey to God. This will be one of the topics we examine in part 3, "Principles for Freedom-Living."

Questions for Personal Reflection or Discussion

➤ How can I transform my suffering into a springboard for personal growth?

➤ What does God's Promise say to me in my present situation?

PART TWO

EMOTIONAL
AND SPIRITUAL
HEALING

7

How Do You Hurt?

Come to me, all you that are weary and carrying
heavy burdens, and I will give you rest. Take my yoke
upon you, and learn from me; for I am gentle and humble in
heart, and you will find rest for your souls.

—MATTHEW 11:28–29

Accepting the reality of suffering in our lives as part of God's loving and still mysterious plan for our lives, a plan that can bring great blessing here on earth and lead us to the fullness of happiness in heaven, is a second step, equally important as the first.

Our step-by-step journey is necessary because God's Promise to bring a greater good out of every instance of suffering is linked intimately to our ability and willingness to collaborate with his plan. God's response to a world that hurts involves you and me. All-powerful and all-knowing, he could do it on his own, but he almost never does. His pedagogy is to involve us in his work of salvation. God didn't free the Israelites from the Egyptians and lead them toward the Promised Land with an overwhelming show of divine power. Instead, he sent the tongue-tied Moses to barter with Pharaoh! Jesus didn't descend to earth on a cloud or with the wings of an angel. He asked Mary if she wouldn't mind carrying him in her womb! The Holy Spirit didn't drop off ten copies of the Bible to the early Christian community. He inspired the authors to pass on, in their own words, what they had heard and seen!

This is God's way. We are part of the Promise.

The difficulty in doing our part is not only a matter of weak faith. I know many faith-filled people who have entered crisis mode when facing personal tragedy. In this crisis they don't lose their faith; they just get stuck. They want to activate their belief and trust in God's power and love, but they are unable. Something is blocking them from tapping into the source of deep inner peace and joy God wants for each of us.

From my experience, these blocks are anything but simple to detect and overcome. Everything we have lived in the past, every one of our moral choices, all of our positive and negative relationships—all these things leave a mark on our psychology. They mold (not "determine") our mind to think, judge, and act in a certain way. Having faith doesn't make all of that history go away; it usually doesn't heal our emotional and spiritual wounds.

The second section of this book deals with our disjointedness. It walks us through how we suffer, why we suffer, and what God can do about it if we let him.

Most of us, given a choice, would prefer to speak of other people's intimacies. It's easy—at times almost irresistible—to talk with a friend about a coworker's inappropriate behavior, the family feuds of the next-door neighbor, an acquaintance's bout with cancer, or our pastor's hypocrisy. Because our own painful issues make us vulnerable (and therefore insecure), we generally find it difficult to talk about them.

In this chapter I want you to come to better understand how you suffer emotionally and spiritually. Maybe it seems ridiculous to spend time on this. After all, if we don't know how we suffer, it would appear we're not suffering in the first place, or at least it's no big deal. And if we know we're suffering, we probably just want to get on with some solutions.

My experience, however, is that many times our obvious emotional pain (loneliness, for example) is both consequence and cause of other sufferings, many of which go undetected. We can be truly free only when we face all of our facts, even the ones that lie under the surface.

For this process to be effective, you have to have an open mind. You have to be willing to see new areas of suffering in your life that you may have passed over until now as unimportant. You have to want to find the weak points in your own emotional and spiritual life, if they exist.

Spotting emotional and spiritual wounds and reflecting on how they influence our way of thinking and acting are very healthy activities. They allow us to open our hearts in a new way to the healing grace of God.

Three Faces of Suffering

We can start by breaking down suffering into what I like to call the three "faces of suffering." They are just general categories. Like a human face, they express a bigger reality—what's going on inside and out. I've also included simple descriptions of each one:

- Physical suffering: experienced directly through our senses

- Emotional suffering: negative sentiments and emotions

- Spiritual suffering: perceived distance from God, real or imagined

No matter what our wounds look like on the surface (of our body or of our soul), we experience them on various levels, and each level affects the others. In human beings, there is no such thing as a one-dimensional malady.

A journalist friend of mine is married to a cardiologist. When I was visiting New York last year, Dr. Mark gave me a tour of the hospital where he was working. It was going through rough financial times, like many of the private hospitals in our country. The hospital board had been forced to bring in an independent management company to try to keep the place competitive with the big conglomerates. Salaries and positions were being hacked, and quality was in jeopardy. Above all, Dr. Mark feared the loss of the personal touch. This was our conversation topic as we walked down one of the sparkling white corridors.

Then I heard barking. A dog? Dogs?! It wasn't just one, or two, or three. It sounded like a kennel. It was. An in-house dog kennel in the main corridor of a New York City hospital! I don't remember the name of it, but it was something like "Rent-a-Puppy." Dr. Mark laughed. I guess he could tell the scene had completely bewildered me. He explained that studies show that patients who spend time with pets—even a "rent-a-puppy"—heal more quickly. Because we are psychosomatic beings (physical, emotional, and spiritual), creating emotional bonds and sharing affection speed up the healing process of our physical ailments.

Later I reflected on this phenomenon and consulted with other doctors. Sharing affection for an animal—or, even better, for and from a human being in a loving relationship—is beneficial because it cures an emotional deficiency in the patient. In this sense, it doesn't heal the physical problem; it heals an emotional one that we may not have known was there, and in turn prepares us to heal all over. When we are emotionally or spiritually weak, our body is off balance and unable to function properly as a whole. When we reestablish the balance, as with an affectionate and wholesome relationship, the body is in a better condition to heal.

Ironically, the pups at this hospital were on the verge of getting the boot by the emergency management team. Budgetary restraints didn't allow for "extras."

Most of us are well aware of this *principle* of interrelated suffering and healing, but we are not so good at recognizing it when we're the subject. We are slow to admit that some of our physical aches and pains and even serious sicknesses may in fact be caused by lingering emotional or spiritual damage. Likewise, we are slow to give sufficient attention to how physical suffering affects our emotional and spiritual being.

Invisible Realities

While the psychological sciences have developed rapidly in recent years, there is still reluctance in some sectors to accept the invisible as real. When people say, "It's all in your head," unfortunately they often mean, "You're making it up," as if physical pain were the only kind that really hurts, and the only kind worth fixing.

Just as dangerous as thinking that psychological suffering is somehow less real than the physical is thinking that everything nonphysical is psychological. We humans are not just physical and psychological; we are spiritual. We are made in the image and likeness of God (Gen. 1:26, Sirach 17:1). We have been created to be united with him here on earth and forever in heaven: "For this is the will of my Father, that everyone who sees the Son and believes in him may have eternal life, and I shall raise him on the last day" (John 6:40). When we get away from God through sin and selfishness, or when we mistakenly think God has distanced himself from us, we suffer spiritually. Neither physical nor emotional remedies will heal a spiritual wound.

Sometimes we fail to give our emotional and spiritual wounds their full due out of ignorance. Other times we do so out of laziness because we know dealing with them (broken relationships, habits of sin, distorted self-image) may be more complex than what we are willing to accept.

A few years ago, one of the young men I teach at the seminary got a call saying his mother had been admitted to the hospital for a serious illness. He got on a plane the same day and arrived at the Mayo Clinic to find his mother in critical condition. The doctors were still unsure of the cause of her recent fainting spells and the seizure that landed her in the hospital. Her blood pressure was erratic, and she showed no signs of fighting for her life. Steve was particularly worried because his parents were going through a nasty divorce. How would his dad respond? Was this how things were going to end? The next day Steve's dad, Bill, came to the hospital to see his wife. At this point Claire had not responded to anyone's voice and barely moved in bed. When Bill walked into the hospital room and greeted Steve quietly, Claire immediately moved her head, as if to see who it was. It was too much: something happened to her vital signs, bells went off, and the nurses rushed in and went into action. Claire made it through the day. Steve convinced his dad that the time wasn't right and that, for the time being, he would take care of his mom and keep his dad up to date on her condition.

Over the next few days Steve stood by the side of his mother's bed. Little by little she began to talk, but her body showed no signs of improvement. The doctors kept her in critical care as they worked furiously to figure out what was holding her down. On the third day Steve decided to broach the issue of the divorce. His mother cried. Little by little he and his mother were able to go through the issues that led to the divorce proceedings, but according to Steve, none of them seemed big enough to have made his mother want to leave his father after so many years. In quieter moments, Steve told his mother about his own vocation, his love for God, and his desire to live his whole life for the good of people's souls. He was trying to make conversation and reconnect with his mother, who now seemed so distant to him because of her rejection of his father.

In the middle of the night on day four, as Steve slept in the armchair at the foot of Claire's bed, he awoke to strange noises. Opening his eyes cautiously, he saw that his mother was sitting up in bed.

"Steve, I need to talk to you," she said. It was her first clear sentence. "I think I know why I'm sick. I have been unfaithful to your dad by seeing another man. I wanted to get out of it, but I didn't know how. Will you help me?"

Claire and Bill are back together, and the doctors still haven't discovered a clear medical explanation for her episode. They do know, however, that from one day to the next Claire got much better. Steve and his mother are convinced that the spiritual and emotional tension she was living under was the cause of her physical breakdown. They have also watched in awe as her physical recovery has paralleled her spiritual conversion. As she progressively let go of her attachment to a double life, she experienced renewed physical and emotional health.

Seven Ways We Suffer

Now we will look very briefly at the ways we suffer. I have identified seven of these. The goal is to paint a more complete picture of the faces of suffering and thus have a clearer picture of our own situation. The seven ways that we examine here are not an exhaustive list by any means. They simply jog the memory and encourage the mind to make connections.

SUFFERING IN TRIFLES

The first taste of human suffering comes in the trifles. These are the little things of ordinary life like discomfort, annoyance, and boredom. They don't turn our world upside down. We put up with them as part of an imperfect world. It may sound trite to even mention little sufferings like these when most of us are dealing with much bigger things, but I think reflecting on how we experience them reveals our general attitude toward suffering.

Discomfort, annoyances, and boredom are just trifles if the rest of our lives are good, but they can torture the discontent. I was on a plane from New York to California, and we were delayed on the runway. The pilot had already made two announcements with estimated times of departure, and the clock had ticked past both. I could see that people were getting fidgety. When the pilot came on the third time with less than good news, the woman in front of me screamed. To tell you the truth, it had a calming effect on the rest of us. We were perturbed, but this woman was out of control. The flight attendant came over to calm her down—bad idea! Flight rage, they call it. The passenger flung her plastic cup with two ice cubes in the direction of the unsuspecting host. That was the end of that. The plane began to move, but not in the direction of takeoff. Police arrived and escorted the now calm passenger off the plane. From all appearances she was a pretty normal lady. She had a laptop. The trifles were just too much.

SUFFERING IN FAILURE AND
PERSONAL LIMITATIONS

Marcela was diagnosed five years ago, at the age of thirty, with multiple sclerosis. MS is a degenerative disease that attacks the nervous system and slowly wipes out cognitive and motor skills. Marcela's first symptoms were chronic tiredness. Eventually she lost the use of an eye, then a leg, and now an arm. She doesn't know what will be next.

"I'm a thirty-year-old in the body of an old woman," she told me.

While I was imagining all the pain she must have, Marcela told me that the physical aspects of her disease are relatively insignificant. What hurts most is the sensation of having lost control of her fate: "I don't know what I'll be able to do later today, or when I wake up tomorrow morning . . . and I certainly don't know what I'll be capable of next month. By far the most difficult thing for me has been coming to grips with having lost the ability to manage even the most basic elements of living."

Suffering in failure and in personal limitations comes at different times for different people. Most of us don't deal with it as early as age thirty, but all of us will face it at some point or another.

Here's a question to ask before the trial comes: Is there any *thing or person* without which I couldn't live happily? If I were to lose my job, reputation, health, husband or wife, power and influence, intelligence, child or friend, athletic ability, or house, would I also lose my inner peace forever?

If we answer yes to any of these possibilities—and most of us would—we have work to do. God wants to bring us to the point of spiritual detachment. It's not indifference or a hardening of the heart. Rather, it is the attitude of the saintly person who loves all things and all people as gifts from God but who never allows any of these to get in the way of our purpose in life—to know, love, and serve God and to collaborate with him to bring with us to heaven as many people as possible.

SUFFERING IN LOST LOVE

It's hard to define love, even when we've experienced it. For those who have found love in their lives—even little vestiges of it—losing it is like dying a thousand deaths. It causes a hole in the heart that's worse than a hole in the head. It's the incalculable loss of the one who knew me—all the good and the all bad about me—and, despite that knowledge, still wanted to be with me, to hold my hand, to defend me and forgive me.

FROM MY IN-BOX

Until that fateful day, I talked to God daily. It was the day I turned forty-three . . . and the day my wife died of cancer. For many months I blamed the Lord. How could he take her? She was so much better than me. At the same time I felt like a hypocrite. Having seen death many times before, I claimed to be well grounded about the journey that we all must make. Yet when it struck my door, I folded like a wet noodle. Many months of soul searching and self-blame followed: "I didn't do enough. I didn't say enough. And damn it . . . I don't need help from strangers to figure all this out." It was a private feud between me and the Lord.

Time heals all wounds, they say. Yeah right! I don't know

who they are, but they don't know squat. The hole in my being is there still. And I expect it to be there for the rest of my life.

—*Shaun*

That's what love is like.

Because love is meant to be reciprocal, when one person balks, the other is in crisis.

FROM MY IN-BOX

Has he forgotten what we've shared? Did the nights really matter? He must be sick, or a little bit mad. Not angry, mad in the head! I gave him everything and he gave it back. At least that's what I thought. He seems to have more to share—he's giving to someone else—but I can't understand how that could be. Was it hidden, or was I just blind?

I want to be angry and I want to hate. But I can't. I love the man, all of him, even the part that denies me now. I don't need his money, his cars, or even his touch. I need him, because he's part of me . . . no, all of me . . . or part of me. Time may tell, but it won't be anytime soon. Thanks for letting me cry with words.

—*Mary Lou*

Love hurts that much because it's what defines us, what makes us fully human. A person who has never loved is bitter and cold because he's confused about who he is and what he's for. A person who loves deeply is happy and warm because he has found a reason for being in giving himself to someone else and being loved in return.

SUFFERING IN SICKNESS

When the doctor enters the room with bad news, we see it on his face. His words are succinct. Mary described to me what it was like for her:

> "Have a seat, Mary. I don't like this part of my job, but. . . . the tests have come back from the lab and you have ovarian cancer. In these advanced stages it tends to spread. There are new therapies that offer considerable hope. I'll be glad to share those with you and your husband when you are ready."

However the news is communicated, sickness is a part of life we have a hard time understanding and digesting. Its random nature makes us question the source: "Who did this to me?" Some point the finger at God. Some blame karma-like fate. "Why now?" "Why me?" or "Why the one I love?"

FROM MY IN-BOX

> I often ask that question as I look at my wife who is suffering . . . again. This time it's an automobile accident, and she has bone fractures in her neck and shoulder. She was just starting to make gains after years of seizures and diabetes. She has suffered since she was a child, malnourished . . . [her ailments] undetected.
>
> —*Sam*

Sickness lays us low. Important things and urgent things all learn to wait or disappear, even lesser sufferings.

FROM MY IN-BOX

I can't believe I got so bent out of shape about those things. Now I just wish I could be well enough to even care.

—*Drew*

In severe sickness, especially when there is no solution in sight, our basest passions—anger, ingratitude, hatred—come to the surface. When we let them get the best of us, our personalities can be transformed almost overnight. We lose the motivation to be the nice, thoughtful persons we used to be.

When Marcela, the young woman with MS, wakes up in the morning, she wonders whether the disease has claimed another limb. Sometimes it's her leg, arm, or even her vision. The concern is not just about her. She wonders who will have to take care of her if she gets any worse. She is a vocalist, and one of her greatest fears is losing the ability to sing. Physical suffering like hers challenges the whole person.

SUFFERING IN THE FACE OF SIN AND WICKEDNESS

Sin and wickedness are hard to look at. They are hard on the eyes because they are ugly, but also because they come in very small print. They hide out as other things and change form. They are hard to pin down.

FROM MY IN-BOX

Is this just me? Could I myself be the origin of this darkness and fear? It can't be me because I am better than that. I used to be better, at least. But then again, now I don't know. Whatever it is, it's got me in its grip.

—*Simon*

Wickedness is an incarnation of evil. It becomes part of our lives when we say no to God and yes to temptation. The Bible tells us that the ultimate incarnation of wickedness is the devil himself. He is the father of lies. We may not have seen him, but we've seen him work. We've felt his presence.

FROM MY IN-BOX

> Why I started, I don't know. I was attracted to darkness. I was already dark—"empty" might be the word—but also dark. I figured that more would be less—more darkness, less pain. I thought maybe the source of darkness, Satan, when added to my emptiness and weakness, could make me strong. It started out just as a game, something to do with older guys who seemed pretty cool. But then it got me, it ate me up. I felt powerful, then weak and sick, powerful, then evil.
>
> —*Jessie*

The devil is wicked, but other things and people are wicked as well. There is a part of us that is attracted to evil. It makes good look bad and bad look good. Acting on that inclination is sin. Sin, the wickedness I freely accept, has consequences. Although we usually choose sin as a way to avoid the suffering of doing what's right, sooner or later sin itself causes us to suffer. When it does, it hurts like nothing else.

I can't think of a single news event with more elements of evil than that of the sexual abuse of minors within the Catholic Church in the United States in the first years of the millennium. For months on end we read and heard daily accounts of disgusting behavior of people supposedly dedicated to God and his Church. Instead these men were taking advantage of their moral authority and leadership positions to seduce young people to satisfy their own base urges.

The widespread failure on the part of administrators to detain predators and protect children was for many people, inside and outside the Catholic Church, even harder to understand.

Wickedness sometimes comes in nice packages. Whether it was fear of the media, a misplaced desire to help recondition the problem priests, or naiveté, nothing can justify the facts. The net result, however, is that the Catholic Church is stronger today because of the cleanup, and children are safer.

I wish the wickedness of sexual abuse were limited to one organization. It's not. Statistics point to family life as the most common place of child abuse, particularly in the homes of stepparents and in foster homes. Teachers are the second-biggest offenders. God help us.

SUFFERING IN MEANINGLESSNESS AND DEPRESSION

In his classic work *Man's Search for Meaning,* the neurologist and psychiatrist Viktor Frankl, an Austrian-born Jew, chronicles his experience in several Nazi concentration camps, where he lost his wife and parents, among others.

Dr. Frankl used his personal experience of living under horrific suffering as an inspiration to study why some people survive what others do not. The data he gathered contradicted traditional sense. In like circumstances of physical and mental torture, some women fared better than men, some elderly better than the young, and some atheists better than the religious. He questioned, he explored, and he didn't take anything for granted. His results were strikingly simple and straightforward: the distinguishing factor between survivors and victims is their ability to find meaning in their existence, no matter how sordid it might be.

Other-centered meaning was the strongest. The weak and infirm who loved someone and pined to see them again always fared better than the indomitable lone ranger who willed his way for personal gain. The mother who accepted her suffering without losing hope for freedom always outlived the prisoner who learned to curse his hopeless fate.

If meaning makes us tick, meaninglessness is already a death of sorts.

FROM MY IN-BOX

I've found out this year that there is no greater pain than having no pain at all. I have everything I could ever want. Incredible! I still remember making the dream list. Though I was just a senior in college, my goals were crystal clear—money, fun, and fame. Unwritten, but just as clear, was an additional request: "power." Now I have it all, at least a bit. And it's not all material; even the family is pretty good, and my health is holding up. But now what? I'm alone with and without people. I'm bored with and without adventure. I'm powerless, with or without control.

—*Steven*

In my experience, the power of meaning is not the same as passion for what I like. It is discovering the reason for *my* living. I'm not going to die for a wife; I'm going to die for *my* wife—the one who would die for me. I'm not going to give up wife and family to become a priest because I like to help people. I'm going to become a priest because I have experienced a call by *Someone* to do something for *him* and for *people with names and faces whom he has entrusted to my care*.

The ultimate meaning in life is being loved by the Ultimate Lover and loving him in return. I can't say I've got this all figured out in my own life. Pride, vanity, ambition, and self-seeking pleasure still distract me from what I know gives me meaning and makes me happy. But curiously, as the years tick by, what I know in my head is making it down to my heart. This doesn't always happen, you know. Old people can be cranky and very unhappy. In fact, the older these people get, the less happy they become. I've seen it in hospitals and nursing homes. That's because there is a center in all of us where we can choose good or bad and where we say yes or no to truth, and that center either blossoms with virtue or rots with vice. Each one of these decisions from within forms us and makes us who we are. The mass murderer doesn't just do bad things; he's morally bad. Mother Theresa of Calcutta was loved for who she was, not just for what she did. The challenge, then, is to build a life, brick by brick, day in and day out—to turn the center of our being into a fortress of goodness and love. This is the preventive drug for meaninglessness and depression.

SUFFERING IN DEATH

In nature everything tends to something—which is another way of saying everything has a purpose. Fins are for swimming, feet for walking, ears for hearing. Ready for this? Among other things, we were born to die.

It sounds harsh because it is. No matter how much faith in God and in the afterlife we may have, the sudden death of a loved one, or confronting our own death, is hard to grasp. It stings. It shocks. It confuses.

Perhaps our mortality doesn't seem right because it's not. God's original plan was for us to live forever, and from that perspective, death is anything but natural. It hurts because it wasn't meant to be.

FROM MY IN-BOX

I prayed and prayed at the hospital that my husband would live, but my prayers were not answered. I just cannot seem to grasp anything about life at all right now. How can I ever find joy in life again without my husband by my side on this earth? Yes, I know he is with me in spirit, but I yearn for his physical presence, his gregarious voice, his tender touch, and thoughtful ways.

—Clare

Father Jonathan, my husband recently died in a bicycle accident from a head injury. It just happened in September, and of course, I am devastated and, yes, looking for an answer. We were each other's soul mate, so why would a good God want to separate a love like ours? I just don't get it. . . . I just cannot seem to grasp anything about life right now. How can I ever find joy on this earth again without my love by my side?

—Pat

The absolute absurdity of death should make us wonder. If everything in nature has a life-perfecting purpose (human development, for example), would those very purposes culminate logically in death? Or is there something more?

If you have loved someone deeply, you will know what I mean; human lore points to the existence of heaven. The longing to be reunited with lost loved ones is so deep within us that I can't imagine God would be quick to disappoint us. Yes, there have got to be consequences for our actions, and even a state of eternal separation from God's love—for those who ultimately and freely turn their noses at God and walk down the stairway of self-separation (hell). But that is so horrific, it's so terribly inhuman and ungodly, that I am confident God's creativity and mercy will be abounding, for each and every one of his creatures. If he was willing to sweat blood and feel abandoned, and to die on a cross for love of our souls, I don't think he'll give up at the hour of our death. He will reach down and show us the five wounds he bore for us. At such a sight, won't we look up at him and ask him to take us by the hand, to purify us, and to let us be with him forever?

The Bigger Picture

At first the seven ways we suffer may seem very different one from the other. In the moment of most intense pain, the cause of suffering is clear. If the cancer would go away, if my husband would come back, if I didn't have this addiction, if I could find meaning in life, and so on—I would no longer be suffering.

But after some time, we see that deep suffering often leaves a common mark. It is the mark of emotional and spiritual damage. It is heart damage, so to speak. This damage is sometimes very evident: "I've lost my faith in God" or "I can't trust anyone anymore." Other times it is not so clear. After passing through trials, broken relationships, or personal tragedies we feel different, and we are different. We may not know precisely what has changed, but spiritual things that used to be easy are now difficult. When people who know us see us acting out of character and don't know how to help, they may say we are struggling with "issues."

The fact is we all struggle with "issues," and we all have heart damage. The damage is the consequence of a mind and heart not completely in tune with God's will. It is the consequence of the ravages of sin, the disordered attachment to doing things our way when we know it's not God's way.

The next chapters are all about solutions, how we can collaborate in God's Promise to bring a greater good out of every instance of evil—in particular, through the healing of the heart.

Questions for Personal
Reflection or Discussion

➤ Do I know how and why I hurt?

➤ Can I see connections between emotional, spiritual, and physical hurt in my own life?

8

Heart Damage

I came so that they might have life and have it more abundantly.

—JOHN 10:10

God's response to our suffering is his Promise to bring forth something even greater than what we have lost and is now out of our reach—health, love, security, and so forth. This response will reach perfection only in heaven, in our eternal embrace of God, but he wants it to begin on earth.

Our point of contact with "life in abundance" is our hearts. It is where we meet God and others and experience love. It follows, then, that if we are spiritually and emotionally wounded, if we have heart damage, part of God's plan to make good on his Promise must be the healing of that heart—the renewal of our God-given capacity and, yes, our willingness to love and be loved.

Because without love we never become fully human, heart damage cramps our journey to personal "fulfillment." I place "fulfillment" in quotation marks because we must be careful not to seek a purely natural happiness. We would be selling ourselves terribly short.

God's plan for us is to be fully united with him in every facet of our being. In simple terms that means we are called to seek God's will in everything and to accept all of his invitations to draw closer to him. It is in this meeting of the wills—our will becoming one with God's will—that we "find ourselves" and where we experience "personal fulfillment." We don't lose our freedom when we give ourselves over to God by doing his will in all things. Because we were made for union with God, in our submission to him we become freer. We share in his divine life.

Another name for this type of union with God is *holiness*. It was never God's intention, believe it or not, that holiness be monopolized by a few spiritual elite. Union with God, doing his will, holiness—this is bare-bones Christianity.

Why are we talking about this? Because a life of simple, down-to-earth holiness—union with God in mind and heart—is the way, the only way I know, to experience the highest levels of meaning, joy, peace, and happiness in the midst of great human suffering.

When God permits us to suffer, he is offering us a hand-delivered invitation to become living saints. It doesn't happen overnight. Bonaventure, a great philosopher and theologian of the thirteenth century and a master of the spiritual life, entitled one of his greatest works *The Journey of the Soul to God* or, in Latin, *Itinerarium Mentis in Deum*. A "journey," a "way," an "ascent," a "pilgrimage"—this is the language of the great doctors of the spiritual life. In our fallen human state we need to work and struggle for holiness. We need to set out on the adventure of Christian living ready for a fight.

Here again we see God's peculiar pedagogy of involving us in his plan. I like Saint James's formulation of God's methodology, as it relates to holiness: "Draw near to God, and he will draw near to you" (James 4:8). God could sweep us off our feet and make us holy from one day to the next, but he has always preferred to wait for us to draw near to him.

Why Is Union with God So Hard?

If God wants us to be holy, and if it's part of his plan for bringing a greater good out of our suffering, why does he make it so hard?

I don't think we can say God makes holiness hard. We make holiness hard by closing off our will to his. When we put our egos on the throne of our lives, God respects our will to push aside his sanctifying presence. When we do this regularly (habits of sin), we deform our minds, hearts, and will and make them less inclined to the things of God.

Structures of sin (deviant social mores, government corruption, indoctrination, media manipulation) and the personal sins of others against us (psychological pressure, abuse, relationship infidelity, scandal) can also make rocky our journey to God. Jesus had tough words for those who led people away from faith: "Whoever causes one of these little ones who believe in me to sin, it would be better for him if a great millstone were put around his neck and he were thrown into the sea" (Mark 9:42).

This reference to obstacles in the spiritual life and in our quest for sense in suffering brings us back to the topic mentioned at the beginning of this chapter—the healing of the heart.

Last night I had dinner with a group of fabulous friends, among them a news correspondent and anchor from one of the major networks. It was a quaint restaurant in the old section of the city—the kind that prides itself in turning down reservations two months in advance and placing so many plates, silverware, and glasses in front of you that you don't know what to do with any of them. But the company was very nice.

During a rare lull in the otherwise energetic conversation, someone brought up the fact that I was working on this book. The table's attention quickly turned to me and my "project." I was reluctant to discuss it in any detail because I know nobody likes to talk about suffering while enjoying fine food.

I explained briefly that I was writing about understanding and living better with suffering. Everyone nodded in agreement about the importance of the topic, but at first it didn't elicit any passionate reactions.

Then one of the quieter members of the group piped up from the far end of the long, rectangular table: "Are you talking about physical suffering?"

"Yes, that too, but I'm focusing on interior suffering caused by emotional and spiritual damage," I replied.

"Damage!?" The exclamation came from the journalist friend who was now sitting on the edge of her seat. She turned, squared off her body, and looked right at me. "Do you have a name for the book yet?" she continued, somewhat rhetorically. I wasn't sure where she was going.

"Well, I'm batting back and forth a few ideas," I replied. "Why do you ask?"

"Well, if you want my suggestion, just call it 'Suck It Up and Move On!'"

We all chuckled. I knew she was an outspoken person, but she still caught me a bit off guard with this forceful comment. "And why is that?" I prodded.

She related how many of her New York colleagues and friends spend up to twenty years with the same therapist trying to deal with their "issues." She said they all talk about "damage" and the "trust factor" but never learn to get over anything. Instead they spend their whole lives in mental shackles because they are "on the mend."

Everyone laughed, including me, as she described with some healthy exaggeration what we all know to be true in some cases. There was something very good about her willingness to throw reliance on therapy to the wind and give proper place to personal responsibility in the project of bettering one's own future.

Sometimes the term "damage" is used as an excuse to revel in self-pity. We will look at "damage" as an issue of the heart—our spiritual core —and set our sights on true freedom.

What Is "Damage"?

My friend wasn't denying the existence of "damage" in people's lives; she was only suggesting a way forward. She would be the first to recognize the power of life experiences to modify negatively the way we experience the present.

There's a time and place for biting the bullet and moving on, but as anyone who has suffered deeply knows, it's not always that easy . . . precisely because there has been real damage. When we are "disjointed" from the inside out, sucking it up and moving on is not always possible, at least not to the degree that we would like.

We should understand "damage" as the weakening of our natural ability to respond appropriately and serenely to life's challenges.

Damage strips our toolshed of the small devices we could ordinarily rely on to fix little problems. When, for whatever reason, our inner world has been turned upside down, beat up, and left incapacitated, ordinary tools just don't work anymore. We reach for them and they aren't there, or they aren't what they used to be. We often don't know why. Damage makes it particularly difficult (but not impossible) to be faithful to lifelong commitments—marriage, for example.

"Just get over it"; "Stop pouting"; "What's your problem?"; "Act like a man [or woman]"; "Toughen up"—these statements all represent good advice, in the right circumstances. But for someone who has suffered serious damage, comments like these are insulting.

They are constant reminders to the one suffering that the person saying them doesn't really know or understand the person with whom he is talking.

Two nights ago I spoke with a guy from Alaska. We had crossed paths several years ago at a weekend retreat in Connecticut. At the time he was dating a girl from Boston who, I found out, later became his wife. They had met on a cruise ship on which he worked as an engineer. She had been touring with a group of old college girl-friends—the last bunch to be single and free to get away—and was taken by this down-to-earth gentle giant. Sandy and Dave must have been about thirty years old at the time, and they fell in love before they realized what it would mean for a northeastern girl, accustomed to the fast pace of a high-level sales job, to uproot everything and move to Juneau, where everything was cold, slow, and uncouth.

Two years into the marriage, Sandy decided she still wasn't ready to raise children in this foreign land, so, to avoid boredom, she took a job that required heavy travel throughout the continental Northwest. On most Fridays she flew back to Juneau.

The marriage fell apart within three years. At this point, I don't know all the details. I do know that Sandy is living with a guy from work. Whatever the case may be, two years after the separation, Dave is still a mess. It's not like him. From what I remember he was fun, carefree, and very even-keeled.

Dave described to me how his life has slowly begun to fall apart over the last two years. "Things are just out of control," he said. He has been able to keep his job with the cruise line, but even there, he told me, he's just hanging on for dear life. He finishes about half the work he used to do, and his boss is catching on. With time, things are getting worse, not better.

I started by talking truth to Dave: "You didn't do anything wrong"; "You've been faithful"; "God is merciful"; "Give it time"; and so on.

From his response I could tell that my words were going in one ear and out the other. He was paying attention to me, but what I said didn't stick. The hurt had pierced another layer of his psyche. His mechanism was out of whack, and the emotions were now irrational. Here there was significant damage.

People who have suffered like Dave may go through regular bouts of disillusionment, anger, bitterness, self-pity, loss of ambition, hopelessness, revenge, depression, and sometimes fear-based panic.

Those who have great faith can sometimes override these natural reactions with supernatural reactions of faith, hope, and love. But when the sadness and pain go deep, even spiritual giants can be taken by surprise. "What happened to my faith?" we wonder.

FROM MY IN-BOX

> Father Jonathan, I feel like such a hypocrite when I go to church. I'm so angry inside. It's so strange because I've always believed in God and I know I have to forgive. I just can't get myself to do what I know I should. I'm separated now from my husband, and I guess it's been about five months, but it seems like a lot longer. He left, and I know it's partly my fault, but I'm telling you, it's mostly his. Whenever we try to communicate, rage builds inside me, and he hates that and just walks away.
>
> —*Megan*

Lest we think, with all my examples about couples, that the best way to avoid interior damage is to simply steer clear of relationships, let us consider the following note, which reminds us of other ways people get hurt.

FROM MY IN-BOX

> It started out so innocently. We did it together, more out of friendship and loneliness than rebellion. And here I am

alone—yes, alone, alone, even with so many around me.
I'm consumed by a craving for what I most detest. Drugs
can't be sin. I don't want them. They have control. But
then there's no real control. Every part of me, in this scary
sobriety, runs wild.

—*Loraine*

Loraine's note reflects a strong physical dependency. She needs professional medical assistance, but, as you can read between the lines, there's more at play here than physical illness. Loraine is suffering emotional and perhaps spiritual brokenness, and this, too, will need healing.

Thank God, human psychology has a way of shutting down our senses to avoid a crash. We put up walls. We learn to cry without shedding tears. But a callused heart and a forgetful mind have pros and cons. On the one hand, they offer us relief from a reality at times too big to confront. On the other hand, they blind us from ongoing damage that may be going on.

Identifying Spiritual Damage

We defined *spiritual suffering* in the last chapter as perceived distance from God, real or imagined. Because we were made to live in union and friendship with God, when we know we have turned our back on him or we feel he has turned his back on us on account of something we have done, we hurt. This hurt usually feels like a guilty conscience.

When the guilt feeling is prodded by recognizing objective wrongdoing (personal sin), it is a very healthy emotion, because it motivates us to ask forgiveness, rectify our behavior, and make restitution. I like to call this kind of good guilt *godly sorrow*. We are mourning our sin.

On the other hand, when the guilt is stirred by nontruths ("God is out to get me"; "God will never forgive me"; "There is no hope for me"), it falls into the category of useless and destructive emotions—specifically, self-pity.

In both cases we suffer spiritually.

Spiritual damage is something different. It is the significant weakening of our spiritual faculties—the ability to pray, ask forgiveness, receive forgiveness, and practice supernatural virtue (faith, hope, and love, for example). Spiritual damage is usually caused by *habits of personal sin*—free and informed choices to reject God's law. Spiritual damage can also be caused by external forces—structures of sin or the sins of others against us.

Consider this note from a reader who clearly has spiritual damage:

FROM MY IN-BOX

Father Jonathan, I read your recent post on forgiveness. It's all nice and I'm sure it has helped some people . . . blessed people . . . people who have never been harmed and have never harmed . . . and probably have no reason to forgive. The person whom I can't forgive is myself. For fifteen years I have carried the burden of taking the life of my unborn baby. My husband doesn't know. The baby wasn't his. It was actually several years before we even met, and I'm sure he would not even care too much if I told him what happened. But I can't. I can't do a lot of things I used to do. My father is an evangelical pastor, and part of me would love to sing in his church again. I just can't look at God and sing. I hear my baby cry every time I try. So I just don't talk to God.

—*Rebecca*

Certainly Rebecca's issues are not only spiritual. Like millions of other women in America and throughout the world who have had abortions, Rebecca endures a deep emotional scar. We would be very mistaken, however, if we blamed her suffering solely on psychological or emotional factors. When we freely choose to reject God's law and Word, we distance ourselves from him. Sin is like a dagger to the soul. Even when we pull it out by reconciling ourselves with God through repentance for our sins, the effects of sin remain (bad habits, broken relationships, and so forth). Only through the grace of God (the healing of the heart) and the strengthening of our will can we gain the degree of spiritual simplicity and freedom we previously enjoyed.

Rebecca needs emotional healing, but first she needs to make amends with God and accept his forgiveness. This is the first step toward complete spiritual and emotional healing, which involves continual renewal of the mind and heart. Had Rebecca turned to God immediately after the abortion, she might still have suffered spiritually and emotionally, but she would not be dealing with the *spiritual damage* she obviously has now.

Identifying Emotional Damage

I don't think I need to convince readers of the existence of emotional damage in our society. We all have it. Sometimes, though, we don't know what it looks like or feels like because it has become so much a part of our daily life. Subtle emotional damage is in some ways even more dangerous than the more obvious kind because we can come to accept it as a natural manifestation of our personality.

Sam was a college student at a university where I worked for a time. He is a super guy; talented, very spiritual, and a lot of fun. But Sam is one of the most indecisive people I know. It drives him crazy. He knows it is a defect, and he wants to change. By his own admission, his indecisiveness is linked to personal insecurity. During a session of spiritual counseling, I asked him why he felt so insecure. "I guess I've always been like that," he said.

"Are you sure?" I responded.

"Why do you ask?" he replied.

"Because you have no good reason to be insecure. You have tons of admirable human qualities. You are smart, athletic, kind, handsome, well liked, and come from a great family. On top of that you have a deep relationship with Christ. You have more reason to have confidence in yourself than almost anyone in this college."

He looked at me, then lowered his eyes for just a second and looked back up. "I know," he said. Then he smiled and chuckled nervously.

Sam knew, but he didn't really know. At one level of his being, he believed what I said; he knew it was the rational answer, and this right reasoning was fortified by his faith in a loving God who had died for him and loves him unconditionally. But he still *felt* insecure and therefore acted in an insecure way, especially in the field of decision-making.

Sam had suffered minor emotional damage. He couldn't live fully according to what he knew was true because his mind and his emotions were constantly telling him something else.

In the next two chapters I am going to give concrete steps for dealing with emotional and spiritual damage. We are going to walk through one way of collaborating with the healing grace of God. I don't want to do that, however, without first defining very clearly how to recognize damage in our lives and how to avoid confusing it with the normal difficulties of a healthy mind and heart.

The key is to avoid thinking that everything we suffer produces long-term damage. Otherwise, we would all be hopeless victims of life. Even people in extreme circumstances sometimes come out of them in great health. Here's an extreme example: if a wife is physically abused on a regular basis by her alcoholic husband, she is going to experience tremendous fear every time he comes home drunk. But the fear is not a sign of emotional damage. In fact, if she didn't experience fear, something would be wrong with her. Her reactions are healthy because they correspond to a real and proportional aggressor, and they move her to protect herself from a real and present danger. Get rid of the aggressor, and the healthy person bounces back. If she doesn't, there is some degree of damage.

The same thing can happen spiritually. Sin truly alters our relationship with God and others. If a man has a habit of viewing pornography, for example, the relationship with his spouse will be affected. If throughout the day he is lusting after other women, there should be no great surprise when his attraction to and intimacy with his wife diminishes. This man does not need emotional counseling. If he wants to feel close to his wife again, he should start by getting rid of the aggressor—namely, the pornography itself.

As in most things, here too we must find the balance between two extremes. On the one hand, we should avoid the temptation to blame all of our present difficulties on damage from the past. On the other hand, we mustn't deny our need for God's healing grace to renew our minds, heal our hearts, and strengthen our will.

Questions for Personal Reflection or Discussion

➤ What do holiness and God's grace have to do with finding meaning and joy in the midst of my suffering?

➤ Have I detected any emotional or spiritual damage in my life? Am I willing to confront it?

9

The Father of Lies

*He . . . does not stand in the truth, because there is
no truth in him. When he tells a lie, he speaks in character,
because he is a liar and the father of lies.*

—JOHN 8:44

I've already made several references to the devil in this book.
His existence and action in the world are a fundamental
teaching of Christianity, even if you don't hear much about
him from the pulpit.

Not long ago I was asked to do some minor consulting for a
Hollywood production that included a scene of exorcism—the
traditional ritual of the Catholic Church in which the properly
appointed minister asks God to release someone from demonic
possession. After being convinced that the director and producers
were interested in portraying the scene in an honest and respectful way, I agreed to offer my advice. (I didn't allow them to use
my name, because I didn't want to affiliate myself with a project

whose content I couldn't control.) We met in a lounge area on the top floor of an old hotel in Rome. The room was dimly lit. A corner of the lounge was set aside for my meeting with the director, the executive producer, and the main actor. We sat on couches around a low marble table. The lounge was sprinkled with other guests, but I assumed we were the only ones in the room involved in the production.

In the initial formalities and salutations, I hoped to get a feel for who I was working with. The lead actor gave me a perfect opportunity when he asked, "So what do we call you . . . 'Jonathan'? 'Father'? . . ."

"If you like, you can call me 'Father Jonathan,'" I responded. It was an opening to ask them about their religious backgrounds. One was "culturally Jewish" and the others were "nothing in particular."

As soon as we sat down, the film director got straight to the point: "Do you believe in the devil, Father Jonathan?"

"Yes, I do," I responded.

"Do you think he can possess someone?"

"Yep, I've seen it. But it's very rare."

"Why so rare?"

"Well, he's usually a bit smarter. He gets involved in our lives under the radar and works ceaselessly to lead us astray, away from God."

Out of the corner of my eye, I noticed there were now two or three people standing not far from our table, almost directly behind me. I signaled their presence to the executive producer. He lifted his hand just off the table as if to say it was all OK.

"And what about you all, do you believe in the devil?" I continued. To my surprise, this group of practical atheists, all of them, responded in the affirmative. The irony hit me: they didn't believe in God, but they believed in the devil! For the next fifteen minutes we talked about the presence of evil in the world. As we did, more and more of those in the room gathered around us to listen in as we sat in our little corner. It turned out that everyone in the room was affiliated with the project . . . and they all wanted to hear and talk about the devil! They knew him because they had felt his presence, they had seen his works.

The great tool of the devil is deceit. He is the Father of Lies, according to the Scripture. We have seen how the pedagogy of God is to involve us in his master plan for redemption. The devil's pedagogy is to make us active participants in our own damnation.

If we ignore the devil's ability to influence our minds and wreak serious havoc on them, we will always be missing an important factor in the equation of emotional and spiritual healing. He is actively working to sow doubt and confusion. The devil's lies do damage!

Here I would like to go back to Sam's story. You'll remember there was no apparent reason for—that is, no real and proportional aggressor to cause—such indecisiveness and insecurity. I asked Sam to reconsider what he had told me earlier about *always being like this*. I suggested he reflect and, above all, ask God to show him the origin of his long-held feelings of inadequacy. Sensing a need for God's grace to heal old wounds, I suggested he ask Christ to remind him of times in his past where these feelings of inadequacy were particularly intense.

He laughed. "I think I can tell you now, even though I don't like talking about it," he said. Sam recounted how he was very popular in junior high school and a solid member of the in crowd. About halfway through the year he became the first guy to have a girlfriend, and she was the prettiest girl in the class. Then one day he came to school and none of his friends wanted to talk to him.

They had simply stopped being his friends. They were jealous of his luck with the girls, and as revenge, from one day to the next they tuned him out. "I couldn't believe it," he told me, obviously moved by the memory. "These guys were supposedly my friends."

Sam's life changed on that day. He shut down on the inside while maintaining an outward presence of being cool and indifferent. He no longer trusted his classmates, girls in general, and, to some extent, even his lifelong friends. The possibility of a similar moment of rejection was enough to make him resolve never to make himself vulnerable to others in the same way again.

Kids can be pretty cruel, but they don't betray people in the same malicious way adults do. If we could watch a replay of what happened to Sam—what his friends actually did and how they executed it—we would surely stand in wonderment at Sam's disproportionate negative reaction. No matter how mean these kids' words and actions may have been, they couldn't possibly merit the life-altering attitude Sam adopted in the wake of the event.

So what happened? I don't know for sure, nor does Sam. But on account of some personal weakness (emotional immaturity, lack of experience, previous damage), he perceived the event in a false way, a way that didn't correspond to reality. He lived the event as definitive and dramatic. In his mind, his relationship with these "idyllic" friends went from perfect to zero overnight.

Now as an adult, Sam saw just as clearly as I did how his original perception of the event was warped. I referred him to Bible passages and good spiritual reading as an aid to renew his mind.

Accepting his internal exaggeration of the event was helpful to Sam, but nevertheless it didn't get rid of the problem. When there is damage, a third person setting the record straight (even when backed by the Bible) can help, but as we'll see, it's usually not enough.

Buying into Lies

I encouraged Sam not to think too much about all of this. Drumming up in our own minds negative experiences from the past is usually not very productive. What I did suggest was that, in his usual time of daily prayer, he dialogue with Jesus and ask him for light and help about every aspect of his life, including this negative experience.

A week later when Sam came back to talk he was very different. He was smiling. He stood three feet in front of me—not the usual ten (a safe distance)—and he spoke with confidence and peace. It was clear he was no longer guarding every word, measuring every response. He put it like this:

"In prayer, when I asked God what he thought about all those negative feelings, it came to me so clearly. Those guys didn't really hate me. They were just being kids. And the uselessness, inadequacy, and all of that—that's not true, either. God made me and he loves me, and that's enough."

Sam recounted this as if it were earth-shattering. But to me it sounded very simple; if I didn't know better, I would say even simplistic. He and I had talked through these very truths he was telling me. He had read all the Bible passages about God's love for him. What happened this time? Why, from one day to the next, did Sam experience an inner peace and freedom he had not felt in many years? God was able to enter Sam's life in an integral way. He was able to speak truth to Sam not with ideas or concepts, but with his healing grace. Because the truths came from God, in the form of grace, Sam experienced real mind and heart renewal.

Let's review Sam's simple journey:

Step 1: He recognized that his feelings were incongruent with reality (that they were irrational) and were somehow related to a past event or series of events.

Step 2: He accepted that the related events from the past were only the occasion, not the cause, of the real damage. (The damage was caused by the lies about himself that he came to believe.)

Step 3: He aided the renewal of his mind and heart by asking for help from someone he trusted and by looking to the Word of God.

Step 4: In prayer, God showed him the specific lies he had accepted and freed him from their bondage.

In moments of particular weakness, pain, or trauma, we are more susceptible to believing nontruths. Our increased sensibility in these moments gives the devil fertile ground for planting his lies deep in our souls.

Mary comes from a great Christian family—upper middle class, several brothers and sisters, and parents who have been happily married for more than forty years. But Mary was always getting sick. Throughout her teenage and young adult years she suffered various physical and emotional illnesses that baffled every doctor who treated her. None of them could find a cause. Some said it was all in her head.

A few years ago, with the help of a good psychologist, Mary began to recall systematic sexual abuse during her childhood by a neighbor. Several independent psychologists concurred that the memories were probably real. Whether the memories were real or not, Mary became increasingly concerned and unstable. She isn't the kind of person to make anything up, to accuse anyone falsely, or to grieve about something that may never have occurred. She was pretty sure, however, that whatever happened was the origin of her other problems. Unless she worked this out, there would be no closure.

The "pain," as she referred to it, came at the most unexpected times: riding the London Underground, talking on the phone with a friend, even sitting quietly in church. Often the pain felt like failure. But it wasn't a failure of the past—the kind that says, "You messed up." It was an existential and permanent failure: "You don't matter." Other times the pain felt like sin: "It's your fault"; "You shouldn't be so nice"; "You lead people on"; "You're dirty"; "You're stupid."

Whatever the feeling of the day, it was always self-accusatory. At the height of her struggle the past, present, and future we're all pretty much the same to Mary: "Because of what happened—or didn't happen—or will happen—I'm always going to be like this, and because I am, I'm always going to make other people suffer."

Mary's road to healing is a happy one, thank God. It wasn't fast, but it was solid, and it has lasted. In Mary's road to healing you will be able to identify the same four steps I used to describe Sam's journey. She lived them in a slightly different order, in a less linear fashion, and because of the depth of the damage, she moved through them more slowly.

Mary brewed in sadness, anger, and despair on account of a ghost from the past. Unwittingly, she had traded in the gift of freedom and self-determination for the right to live in perpetual misery . . . because *someone else* had entered and taken control of her life.

Mary came to me out of desperation. Psychologists and therapists had helped her in a respectful and nonmanipulative way to recall the sexual abuse. She was relieved to have pinpointed the start of her interior confusion and pain (that is, the damage).

This was step one. She had identified the related event. But the pain had not gone away. Was she going to have to live like this forever? As we talked through her story, it became clear she had already made significant progress. She recounted how at first she had looked for inner peace in the abuser's eventual repentance or acknowledgment of wrongdoing. With the good advice and help of professionals, she put that false hope aside as unhealthy and unrealistic, not only because it may never happen, but, most important, because even if it were to happen, it wouldn't completely heal the wounds.

In talking to Mary, I could see she had a truly beautiful soul. Her suffering was particularly deep because she had once experienced the beauty of emotional and spiritual wholeness. She longed to recover the innocence of her early childhood and the harmony of her family life.

"What is the hardest thing in dealing with all of this?" I asked her.

"It's the pain that comes out of the blue," she replied.

"What do you mean by 'pain'? Is it physical?"

She didn't need to think long to give an answer. She had obviously done plenty of thinking. "Yes and no," she said. "I feel it coming on, sometimes like a hot dagger, sometimes like a slow fever, and usually like a quick, cold jolt. But I know the pain isn't caused by anything physical because it comes out of the blue, and in all different circumstances."

I could tell that Mary was besieged by lies about herself.

"After the pain leaves, how do you feel?"

"I feel like I always do, but just more intensely, I guess—worse."

"And how does that feel?" I continued.

Mary lowered her glance. "I feel like I'm dirty, useless, and alone."

"And are you all those things?" I replied.

"That's how I feel," she said, and then she cried.

Because I knew Mary's family and I was beginning to get to

know her as well, I knew that none of what she *felt* was true. She wasn't dirty, she wasn't useless, and she wasn't alone.

For the next several months we worked on identifying the lies for what they were. We weren't looking to get rid of them just yet. Mary knew on an intellectual level she had done nothing to become "dirty," she had many gifts and talents to offer the world, and she was surrounded by family and friends who loved her dearly. But when she felt the pain . . . there was the lie.

It was hard—almost impossible at first—for Mary to think the pain did not cause the dreadful thoughts, but rather that it was the thoughts—fear induced by lies about herself—that caused the pain. Psychological stimulants, often uncontrollable, were provoking subconscious fears . . . fears of dirtiness, uselessness, and loneliness, among others. Mary didn't experience any of this as fear. For her it was just pain . . . a quasiphysical pain of some sort. She described the unpleasant feelings that followed the pain as shameful statements of truth about herself. Only later did she come to understand these "post-pain" feelings as residue from the same work of the lie-induced fear.

One simple practice that helped Mary, and has helped many others, was to examine the dynamics of her mind and heart as soon as possible after the actual experience of fear and pain. I suggested she keep a disposable journal. She learned to be attentive, when she felt the fear and pain coming on, to the accompanying lie. She wrote down each phrase in a little blue notebook. I suggested she title it "The Little Book of Big Lies."

Over time we talked through each flagrant lie in that little book. I asked her where the thoughts came from, whether she believed them, and if she wanted them to control her mind.

Mary didn't know where they came from; she didn't really believe them (at least, not intellectually); and no, she didn't want them to have free reign in her life.

Next to each line in her book we together wrote down the real deal about who she is and why she is of inestimable worth, a worth that can never be destroyed. For the next few months, Mary replaced the spontaneous bad thoughts with the truths we both believed.

We decided to use Bible passages to call to Mary's mind fundamental truths about herself, God, and others.

This was step three. She asked for help from someone she trusted and looked to the Word of God for light.

I have no friends. . .

"I no longer call you slaves, because a slave does not know what his master is doing. I have called you friends, because I have told you everything I have heard from my Father" (John 15:15).

Nobody really knows me for who I am. . .

"Before I formed you in the womb I knew you, before you were born I dedicated you" (Jer. 1:5).

Nobody loves me. . .

"Because you are precious in my eyes and glorious, and because I love you, I give men in return for you and peoples in exchange for your life" (Isa. 43:4).

It's all my fault. . .

"For freedom Christ set us free; so stand firm and do not submit again to the yoke of slavery" (Gal. 5:1).

I'm dirty from the inside out. . .

"What God has made clean, you are not to call profane" (Acts 10:15).

Things will never get better. . .

"I have grasped you by the hand; I formed you, and set you as a covenant of the people, a light for the nations" (Isa. 42:6).

Weeks passed and I didn't hear from Mary. When she finally called, I could hear in her voice that something had changed. In particular, she told me she now realizes that somewhere along the line she came to believe that her present and future happiness depended entirely on "fixing" what this man had done to her. "That's not true!" she told me now. "He didn't change me at all. If I live in the truth of who I am and why God loves me, I can take back the reins of my life."

This was step two. She recognized that the related event was only the occasion, not the cause, of the long-term damage.

The real damage was caused by the lies she came to believe about herself.

Mary now had new serenity. She told me how she had memorized each of the six passages we had selected in my office and how, instead of waiting for the "pain" to come and replacing the accompanying lie-induced thoughts with the biblical truth, she just started repeating the verses in her head whenever she had a free moment. It started out as mere repetition, she said, but it became prayer. Over and over again she talked to God . . . not in her old, convoluted thought pattern, but rather in truth.

I was happy for Mary, and I told her so. But before we hung up, I told her I didn't think this would be the end of her pain. Though I believe in the power of God to work miracles in any way he wants, God's grace and power ordinarily work through natural mechanisms. After all, he created these psychological, spiritual, and physical mechanisms for a purpose, and that, too, is a miracle.

Simply replacing lies with truths (even biblical truths) can help someone establish a semblance of stability in their lives and is a necessary step toward full mind renewal. But when there is deeply seated damage, *knowing* the truth is rarely enough to achieve a full renewal of the mind and healing of the heart. God needs to step in and work a miracle of grace.

Mary agreed that things probably weren't all in order. She still couldn't imagine having an intimate relationship with a man, for example. By passing through steps one, two, and three (though not in that order), she was better prepared for God, in prayer, to heal her heart of the lies that were so deeply embedded there.

Sam's road was relatively quick. Mary, on the other hand, was not yet able to hear so clearly the voice of God, because the lies were so deeply embedded in her psyche.

In the next chapter we will discuss more specifically the dynamics of lie-induced behavior and feelings (like Sam's and Mary's) and how to discover the source of the specific lies that keep us down. The conclusion of Mary's story will be part of this next chapter.

Questions for Personal
Reflection or Discussion

➢ What lies have I accepted that have left emotional and spiritual damage?

➢ What am I going to do to begin replacing lies with truth?

10

Sourcing the Suffering

Do not conform yourselves to this age but be transformed by the
renewal of your mind, that you may discern what is the will of
God, what is good and pleasing and perfect.

—ROMANS 12:2

You may remember the frightening story of an eleven-year-old Missouri boy, Shawn Hornbeck, who was kidnapped and held hostage for over four years. The bits of public information about the case that have surfaced through interviews and the court case itself paint a terrifying picture of what life must have been like for this young boy during those long months and years of captivity under the watch of his kidnapper.

The story was not only frightening; it was also fascinating. When Shawn was found by the police in January 2007 after another young boy had gone missing and new clues pointed to their mutual captor, he looked like any other Middle American fifteen-year-old. In fact, his body piercings, shaggy hair, and baggy clothes made him look so much like an ordinary fifteen year old that media speculation started to call into doubt his victim status.

Equally disturbing was the "normal" life Shawn seemed to have lived during those years. His alleged kidnapper, Michael Devlin, worked hard to maintain a public profile of normality. Neighbors noticed nothing out of the ordinary with the "father and son" pair. They said Shawn used to ride his bike in the streets, play with friends, and use a cell phone. Internet reports even show that "Shawn Devlin" created his own Web pages and roamed the World Wide Web.

Why didn't Shawn ride his bike to the local police station, whisper his secret to a neighborhood friend, call 911 on his cell phone, or cry out for help on the Internet? He certainly had plenty of time on his hands, as his captor apparently left him home alone during the day while he was at work.

The touching images of a smiling Shawn in his parents' arms after the rescue leave no doubt about the boy's relief to be in his real home again.

But they also highlight how fear can manipulate the human psyche and paralyze our ability to act in accord with truth. Shawn longed to be with his parents and had plenty of chances to escape, but, by his own admission, he was terrified for his own safety and his family's if he were to make a break.

I spent the morning of January 13 (the day after Shawn was found) on the phone with doctors and psychologists whom I trust, reflecting on similar cases of fear-induced, irrational behavior I have encountered in my ministry.

On account of the sexual and physical abuse he endured (now very public information), when Shawn looked down the street at the police station not far away, he didn't picture freedom; he pictured his captor and what the punishment for being caught would be. The mere thought paralyzed him.

I received hundreds of e-mail messages from people saying they couldn't understand this. Their line of argument was that for Shawn it shouldn't have been a question of how bad the punishment would have been, because at age fifteen he must have known he could have easily made it to the police station without his captor catching him. After all, his captor was at work all day!

This is the naked truth about human psychology: we are weak and susceptible to manipulation by nontruths.

Whether our irrational behavior is the result of a psychological survival mechanism kicking in, as is most likely Shawn's case, or, as in the majority of cases, the result of accepting lies promulgated by the enemy of our soul—the devil—the result is similar. We act according to what we believe is best for us, even when it isn't.

If someone had been there with Shawn during those long days when he was at his captor's home alone, he could have helped Shawn see why he really had no reason to fear an escape: the door was open; the police station was nearby; his captor was miles away; Shawn was young and quick; and so forth.

Reminding Shawn of these things may have been sufficient to shed light on the whole list of nontruths he had come to believe. He could then have dealt with each of them. I can imagine what Shawn's responses would have been: "Oh, so you are telling me when I get to the police station, Michael really won't be able to find me again?"; "And the police will really protect my family, too?"

Shawn's case is extreme, but the internal dynamics are remarkably similar to those of much more ordinary cases of emotional damage. The one major difference is that the more ordinary the case and the further we are from the moment of the traumatic event, the more difficult it is to discover the list of nontruths that are dictating our irrational behavior. The source of Shawn's irrational behavior was his captor, Michael Devlin, and the lies he had fed to this disjointed youth. In much more ordinary ways, we too can believe lies told to us by others or suggested to us by the devil. The dynamics are remarkably similar.

Trauma, Big or Small, Makes Us Susceptible to Lies

I would like to give another example of identifying the lies in our lives that cause us to suffer. Like Shawn's story, this one illustrates the power of lies to affect the way we view our present reality. I hope it also underlines how moments of trauma, big or small, make us susceptible to believing lies. The following example is certainly less dramatic and much closer to home.

Parents have a sixth sense for shielding their kids from themselves. My dad is a man of principles. He's a loving man. He's a holy man. And I always thought he was a perfect man. Last year he told me he was not.

If I remember well, it happened in Seven Hills, a little suburb on the west side of Cleveland, Ohio, where Dad grew up. As in many parts of the Midwest, here high school football claims as many fans as the NFL. The neighborhood pickup games were played on the high school practice field, and, unlike the manicured carpet reserved for Saturday-morning home games, this one was bumpy, hard, and mostly dirt. School was out, and erstwhile freshmen were now cocky sophomores. At five feet two inches and a whopping ninety-eight pounds, Dad had little chance of making varsity. But he was quick and had good hands. It was third down. Neighborhood rules said two completions were required for a first down. Jim wasn't quarterback, but he always called the plays: "First a down-and-out and then a button-hook" (a little pass play where you stop on a dime). Dad stopped and the ball came. Lights out. Danny Herrera was big, real big, and not the merciful kind.

When Dad told me this story, his eyes filled with tears. He used to never cry. Now, in his wise years, he cries with dignity and ease. According to Dad, Danny Herrera influenced, unfortunately, the next fifty years of his life. When the lights turned back on in the high noon sun, Danny was still looking down—down at little Bob: "You're a squirt, Bob. You can't play with the big boys." When Dad looked up and heard those words, something snapped inside. He believed a lie: "I'm a squirt . . . and that means I'm useless as a man unless I can prove otherwise."

In the moment Dad didn't even realize he had made such an ir-rational conclusion. A rational one would have been "Yeah, Danny's right. At five-foot-two and ninety-eight pounds, I shouldn't play with these guys anymore." But instead he took the experience out of its proper context.

Believing the lie meant *reacting* to someone else's narrow view of him rather than living according to what God thinks. Soon after the football game, Dad decided that from that moment on, academics and career success would be the way to find self-worth. He would be a success through good grades, college, law school, money, and politics. They would be his road to personal fulfillment.

Now, those aren't bad things, and quite honestly, when I was growing up I always thought they were pretty good. But Dad ex-plained to me how bad they were *for him.* They were his way of looking for self-worth in material things, which inevitably corrode and perish. His ambition wasn't so much a way to live up to a healthy challenge or make use of his talents for the good as it was a way to get back at the "big guy" Danny represented, and especially a way never to taste defeat.

Living to avoid defeat is a sure way to miss out on at least part of the great adventure of living a life of freedom—what I like to call *freedom-living.*

As he ended the story, Dad told me he now realizes that his choice to change the playing field from football to academics and career was only a temporary escape from the lies he had swallowed about his self-worth.

Dad was able to tell me this story because he had already experienced significant healing. In prayer Dad allowed God to take him back to the different moments in his life of big or small trauma—including this one on the football field—in which he had accepted lies about himself, God, and others. He asked Christ to speak truth to him about those experiences. He soon began to experience a new-found freedom and joy that comes from knowing, in spiritual and emotional wholeness, the truth about ourselves and God's personal love for each one of us.

I promised to come back to Mary's story. We left off when she was just beginning to regain a semblance of control over her emotional world. She had learned to replace the nontruths that caused her so much pain with God's Word. She reported an acceptable degree of stability, but we both agreed she was not completely better.

This is the status of millions and millions of our contemporaries. Through one technique or another, we learn to get by. We become professionals at dealing with the background music of serious discontent. Faith helps some people. Others depend on distractions.

I told Mary I thought there was still a part of her heart and mind that God's healing grace had been unable to transform. Unable? Yes, so to speak. God usually holds back his power out of respect for our free will and our natural (God-given) mechanisms. Without our even asking, he could at any moment wipe us clean of any trace of emotional damage. But he doesn't usually do this. He wants us to be intimately involved in our own healing: "Ask and it will be given to you; seek and you will find; knock and the door will be opened to you" (Matt. 7:7).

Mary had asked, searched, and knocked many times. Where were the answers? Why did the door remain shut?

I don't think the door was shut. Mary just wasn't well enough to walk through it. Part of God's incredible patience with us can be seen in his respect for our natural healing mechanisms. It is easy to see this with physical healing. Doctors use the gift of intelligence to study medicine. They, in turn, teach us how the body works and how to get better. It would be presumptuous to ask a doctor to make us well even as we eat junk food, avoid all exercise, and disregard our medical prescriptions.

It is not altogether different with emotional healing. God respects our psychological mechanisms. When these mechanisms have been violated by poor development or trauma, psychologists and psychiatrists can help us get better through natural means. But as we have already alluded to, we must also keep in mind that our psychological and emotional world is the devil's playground: "Your opponent the devil is prowling around like a roaring lion looking for someone to devour" (1 Pet. 5:8).

Purely natural techniques don't heal supernatural wounds. We need the grace of God.

Medical professionals can point out where and how our psyche has been injured and can offer many helpful techniques for natural healing. But if we leave out of the equation negative, supernatural forces (the devil and his lies) that bind our psyche and keep us down, we will always be slow to turn to positive, supernatural forces (God and his love) to free us from our bondage.

Cases like Mary's, where a person's psychology has been severely damaged through the trauma of sexual abuse, are some of the devil's favorite targets. The aggression against the victims is objectively so terrible that he can lob lies in their direction and those lies almost always stick.

We tend to forget that the "glue" that binds these devilish lies to the victim's mind is not natural. Because it flows from the devil, it is a supernatural substance. It only makes sense (and this has also been my experience) that the most effective solvent be supernatural as well (the healing grace of God). This is the "second stage" of mind renewal.

When I explained these principles to Mary, a light bulb went on inside her. Her experience with many good psychologists had taught her to be a survivor. But her struggle didn't go away. She was still stuck to the past.

I asked her if she wanted to be truly free. I asked her if she was willing to let go of the past and experience continual freedom-living in the present.

These questions are essential, because we can get used to being a victim, and if we don't want freedom God won't force it on us. We can become accustomed and even attached to our suffering. We wonder who we would be if we didn't have to deal with this or that issue. God will never free us if we choose to stay stuck.

Mary told me she wanted God to renew her completely.

Keeping in mind the supernatural realities, I told Mary my hunch was that it would be helpful if she were to invite God in prayer to show her precisely what was holding her down, and to do this in a certain way. Through the help of good psychologists, Mary was ahead of the game. She didn't need to pinpoint the related event. She knew the traumatic event of sexual abuse that was the starting point of her long suffering. What she still may not have known, I suggested, was why that distant event still had power over her. As I had done with Sam, I suggested she take more time for prayer and invite God to help her relive those hurtful moments from the past in his presence and truth. I encouraged her not to be afraid to actually feel again what she felt back then, if that's what God wanted.

As with Sam, I suggested that she then dialogue with Christ about what she was feeling, and, in particular, invite him to show her what he thought about the event itself and the corresponding feelings.

Mary reported to me that the first time she prayed like this, she experienced peace like she had never known before. She didn't get any miraculous visions or even learn any new truths about her situation. But it was through reliving, in the presence of Jesus and on an intellectual and emotional level, the terrible moments of her past that a new spiritual freedom was released in her. She had asked God for help many times before, but she had never opened her heart to him in such a complete way.

In prayer she experienced with certainty of faith that, in her words, "God was with me even in the moment of abuse and he is with me now. I am not alone." Over several months, every time something would "trigger" the pain, she would look for a quiet place to pray . . . even for just a minute or two. She would turn those feelings from the past or the present over to God and ask him what he had to say about them. Sometimes she heard God speak new truths to her: "I love you"; "Trust in me." But most of the time she just stayed in his quiet presence. Each time she turned to him with her whole being, God was healing her heart.

Many months later, Mary is still in awe of how the things that used to trigger the "pain" now come and go with almost no effect.

What I have described here, in Sam's and Mary's case, is not a psychological tool for "memory recall." It is allowing God to work in our lives in an "integral" way—that is, in our spiritual, intellectual, and emotional worlds. With no suggestive or manipulative interference from anyone, God can use the mechanisms of memory and emotion that he created to bring to our minds events from the past that are related to our present emotional and spiritual suffering. When we open those areas we have kept hidden, God enters and heals.

What I'm describing is not so much a new method of prayer and recovery as it is a simple deduction from what we already know through human experience and Christian doctrine. I'm inviting you to tap into the way God made us. By following these principles, we are preparing our natural mechanisms of the mind and emotions to be open to the very "ordinary" miracle of complete mind renewal.

How Do I Know It's Really God Talking to Me?

If proper interpretation of Scripture is essential in order to understand the full meaning of God's Word (as we discussed earlier), even more important is proper discernment in our own prayer, because here there is more room for subjective error. What if Sam and Mary, for example, had "heard in prayer" that God didn't really love them? What if they had come back with an even deeper conviction of their *uselessness,* this time "seconded by God himself"?

Because we are spiritually hard of hearing, we can make mistakes. Sometimes we think we hear God's voice, and we simply get it wrong.

How do we recognize and discern God's voice? I recommend three things to start:

1. Read and contemplate Sacred Scripture.

2. Study sound Christian doctrine.

3. Ask for guidance from a prudent and holy person who will speak the truth to you even when it hurts.

The writings of the Christian psychologist and counselor Dr. Edward Smith (a southern Baptist) and of Fr. Dave Tickerhoof (a

Catholic priest who builds on Smith's writings) have confirmed and shed light on the spiritual principles I have described here.

Dr. Smith has developed a "prayer methodology" that involves a trained counselor accompanying another person as that person seeks help from God to source the lies that have caused inner damage. Smith insists that this method should never involve suggestive or manipulative coaching. The leader simply invites the person to ask God for help in "following the smoke" from the present negative emotion (anger, fear, resentment, and so forth) to emotions of a similar feel from the past.

Smith and Tickerhoof both explain how God has wired our minds in such a way that emotions of related events "feel" the same. We can use the natural mechanisms of the brain to "follow the smoke" from a negative emotion of the present to a related emotion and its corresponding event from the past.

If we allow ourselves, explains Smith, and especially if we ask God for his help in prayer, we will remember moments in the past that "felt" similar to the negative emotions we are dealing with in the present. Related events have "matching feelings," even if they are years apart. If a woman, for example, is gripped with fear every time her husband gets up and walks away silently from a heated conversation, in prayer she can ask God to show her moments from her past in which she had similar feelings of fearful abandonment. She will usually find that her husband is not causing the extreme fear; rather, his actions are "triggering" existing fears from the past. By "following the smoke" in prayer, she can pinpoint this unresolved damage.

Smith insists this is not an exercise of therapeutic memory recall. It is allowing the God-given mechanisms of the mind to point to related events.

In theory, this is much like what we described in chapter 8, "Heart Damage," and what we have described in the current chapter. What is new in Smith's approach is the method of pinpointing the connection. He uses the natural mechanism of "following the smoke" to cooperate with God in his desire to indicate to us what event from the past is related to the current difficulty.

A second step of Smith's methodology involves confronting the unresolved damage. Once the person has pinpointed the related event, the trained counselor encourages the person to relive that moment and its corresponding emotions and to talk with the counselor about what he is feeling. Then the counselor invites the person to ask God what *God* thinks of that past event (again, without making any suggestions or insinuations about what God's opinion on the matter might be).

Many people who have followed this prayer methodology with the aid of a trained professional have experienced marvelous healing as God reveals his truth and renews their minds and hearts.

Whether you find this particular prayer method helpful will depend greatly on your background and spiritual sensibilities. It seems of particular relevance in cases where inner damage is so severe that a person is unable on his own to penetrate his emotional barriers.

Regardless, I think some of the underlying principles of this method are solid and can be helpful to all of us in our personal prayer. These principles, again, are as follows:

- With the help of God we can easily discover the connection between disproportionate negative emotions surrounding a present difficulty and related events from the past by "following the smoke"—that is, recalling, in prayer, emotions of the same "feel".

- When we allow God to speak to us about these past events, on a spiritual, intellectual, and emotional level, his word of truth comes with healing power.

As in most things, there is a danger here of placing too much importance on our feelings, on past events, and on spiritual and emotional damage. We can start thinking and acting as if everything we feel, believe, and do is dependent on or even determined by the past. This is not true.

It is important to find a balance between seeking healing of the wounds that are holding us back on the one hand, and leaving the past behind us and moving forward in faith on the other.

Part 3 is about moving forward in faith in the adventure of freedom-living.

Questions for Personal Reflection or Discussion

➤ Do I want God to enter my soul and heal me in an integral way? Will I open myself up to him in prayer?

➤ Am I giving God and his grace their proper role in my spiritual life, or am I trying to do it all on my own?

PRINCIPLES FOR FREEDOM-LIVING

11

Making a Fundamental Option for Holiness

Be renewed in the spirit of your minds, and put on the new self,
created in God's way in righteousness and holiness of truth.

—EPHESIANS 4:23–24

Part 3 presents principles that can help us live free from the bondage of senseless suffering. These principles help us cooperate better with God's sanctifying grace through the strengthening of our will. They introduce us deeper into a life of freedom-living.

What Is My Idea of Success?

If my idea of success is out of sync with God's perfect plan to bring me to life in abundance, I will be forever frustrated. I will be spinning my existential wheels.

The goal of this chapter is to invite you to make a *fundamental option for holiness*. It is our first principle of freedom-living, a decision to align our idea of personal success with God's purpose and perfect plan for our lives.

We have been created to praise, revere, and serve God our Lord, and by this means to collaborate with his grace in the salvation of our souls. The other things on the face of the earth are created for us that they may help us in pursuing the end for which we have been created. It follows that anything that gets in the way of God's purpose and plan for us should be avoided as a distraction from our journey to God.

The Christian's fundamental option shouldn't be confused with a moment of conversion, although at times the two can happen simultaneously. It involves inviting God to take the throne of *every aspect of our lives*. Our fundamental option is a decision, or set of decisions, we make at the deepest core of who we are to build a life around holiness. On account of human immaturity, some Christians never make this fundamental option and try to straddle two worlds. They come up short and disappointed—all the rules, but none of the joy that comes from total self-abandonment to God's will.

If you have already made a fundamental option for holiness, I would invite you to use this chapter to renew your decision and to ask God to strengthen your resolve. For those who haven't, these pages will be a summary of what making this option entails.

Christ-Centered Living

The apostle Paul, after enduring torture, imprisonment, shipwreck, calumny, and much more, expressed better than anyone else what the result of the full equation for life in abundance looks like: "For to me life is Christ, and death is gain" (Phil. 1:21).

What is it about Paul that he can speak and act with such confidence? How can he be seemingly indifferent to pain and even death itself? If you read his words again, the answer is there: "For to me to life is Christ, and death is gain." Paul wasn't naive or indifferent, but he had come *to prefer union with Christ over everything else.* He came to know Jesus Christ in such a profoundly personal and intimate way that he was saturated with his love. When he says his "life is Christ," he means that his life, and everything he does, is all about loving and being loved by Jesus. Paul is a man who lived consistently with his fundamental option.

This is the wholeness God wants for us. This is the source of the inner peace and meaning for which we long. The fundamental option for holiness requires going beyond the book knowledge as described in chapters 4 and 5 and letting God be God *in our lives,* just as Paul did in his.

Maybe the apostle Paul's life ideal—"My life is Christ"—sounds a bit boring. What about going to the ball game? Would this spiritual transformation mean the end of good food, vacation, and generally having a good time? Not at all. But some think it does. Here's what 60 *Minutes* correspondent Morley Safer wrote in CBS News's weekly newsletter, "C Note," about his New Year's resolution:

"I resolve to never make resolutions. My sins are all pleasurable, my virtues impeccable. I love animals, small children and I am never cruel to grown-ups, unless it is absolutely necessary. I smoke too much and occasionally over-medicate on good red wine. Saints are the most tedious people, humorless and lacking in imagination. I have no intention of ever becoming one."

I assume Safer (a very good journalist, by the way) wrote this tongue in cheek. But I meet people all the time who say things like this because they mean it. Christianity for them is about rules to keep, and they fear that these boundaries will hold them back from doing what they want. They are looking for lasting happiness, and they don't want anything to get in their way. I don't blame them. In fact, happiness is what we all pine for naturally, and if this is natural, then it comes from God and is very good.

The trouble is that sometimes we don't know what will make us happy. We get it wrong. Jesus came to tell us what it is that leads to deep and lasting happiness: "I am the way and the truth and the life. No one comes to the Father except through me" (John 14:6). He also told us what gets in its way: "The wages of sin is death" (Rom. 6:23).

Let's look at this from a different angle. Have you ever longed, hungered, to be loved more deeply? I talked to a woman today who suffers deeply because she yearns to be loved by her husband in a way she can really "feel." But instead she just "feels" his distance and his anger. She certainly isn't the only one who suffers this emotional loneliness.

As a child, did you ever hunger to be loved deeply? As a single adult? As a married lover? Have your hopes ever been dashed? Have your expectations for such love led you to feeling betrayed by a parent who turned out to be awfully imperfect, by a friend who didn't stand with you when you needed him most, by your spouse, or even by someone you held in high esteem who let you down, failed you, or even abandoned you? It makes you want to lose faith in mankind!

The expectations we have for "perfect" love flow from a very strong and real intuition, one that is at the center of our being. It is a sense there must exist "perfect love." We have a vague picture of what it must feel like and what it must look like. Poets write about it, artists compose songs about it, Valentine's Day advertises it, and some very happy people give us hope it is for real.

But then we remember, almost ashamedly, that we ourselves are not perfect. We can try to love perfectly, but we fail. Our imperfection is a part of our human nature. Our bodies wear out, we hurt people easily, we make mistakes, we lose jobs, and sometimes we just aren't very nice. By experiencing our own limitations and seeing them in others, sooner or later we come to grips with the truth: human love will always disappoint us. It will never match up to our expectations.

But the good news is very good. Our longing to love and be loved, in a perfect way, is God-given and therefore has a purpose: to keep our hearts restless until they rest in God. As Augustine of Hippo wrote in his *Confessions,* "My heart will be restless, until it rests in thee."

Our longing for more love than what humans can give and receive can lead the honest soul to love the Perfect Lover. His love is so deep and amazing it will fill our hearts to overflowing. He promises to be our hope and our purpose in life. He will also teach us the art of loving others and receiving graciously imperfect love in return.

Experiencing God's personal love for us can transform our hearts and renew our troubled minds. It can drench our wounded souls with healing grace and implant in our hearts a new trust that will not disappoint. When we draw closer to this perfect love, our souls take on more of his nature, and our love becomes more divine—more faithful and true and humble and honest.

The apostle Paul and many others like him in his day and ours are a living testimony that this perfect love is within our reach. Because a saint (someone particularly close to God) loves and experiences the love of God more than the rest of us, he is fundamentally happy. He is the one with the most inner freedom. He laughs easily at himself and often with others. He is the one most sensitive to and most grateful for the goods of this world while never losing focus on the hope of the world to come.

That sounds quite different from Morley Safer's description of a saint being tedious, humorless, and lacking in imagination.

Why All the Rules?

Every new car comes with an owner's manual. If we want the car to run well, we should use the manual. God created us. He knows us. And because he loves us, he has given us an owner's manual for life. It gives us guidelines to discern which things eventually are going to do us damage and make us unhappy—and vice versa.

FROM MY IN-BOX

I moved in with my boyfriend after about six months of dating. I was raised Catholic and knew that, for some reason, I wasn't supposed to do that. But since I didn't really know why (I don't care about rules for their own sake), and because everyone else here in Canada does, I figured there was no reason not to. I liked him a lot, and figured this would be a good way to find out. My grandmother almost had a heart attack, but she couldn't tell me why it was wrong . . . and neither could my parents. But now I know why! It's so simple it's scary. When you share everything, including your sexuality, there's no more to give, and there's no more to get. I love this guy, and I think he loves me, but he tells me he's not sure if he wants to get married. Why should he? He's got everything he wants without any commitment! That can't be true love. Why doesn't anyone ever explain to people like us out here in the real world why the Ten Commandments aren't so bad after all?!

—*Courtney*

The owner's manual is not just for us; it's also for the good of the people around us and those who depend on us. Sin is always social. When we think we know better and go against the owner's manual, we wreck lives. The following e-mail message should be enough to make us hate sin forever.

> I had no safe place as a child, no place free from being slapped in the face, choked, punched, beaten, and molested. As I grew up I grieved for the "loss" of the mother and father that I should have had. My teenage years were angry and I was withdrawn. I was left with that lingering realization that I was not lovable, worthless. I suffered depression and survived bulimia, even while the consciousness of all that I could not "control" was destroying me.
>
> —*Maureen*

What were Maureen's parents thinking? In their sick minds, they were looking for happiness in all the wrong places.

"But I thought sin was an offense against God," you may say. It is. But if we don't know God personally, and we think sin is *only* about offending God, there's never going to be much motivation to avoid it. Besides, we wonder how anything *we* could do could ever affect someone so big and so far away.

Our sin doesn't offend God the way a mean look or sarcastic comment would offend a friend. Nothing we do can add or take away from his perfection. Our sin is an offense to God because he loves us, wants the best for us, and is sad to see us reject his perfect plan for our happiness. He is especially sad when we reject his forgiveness and mercy and in this way risk separating ourselves from him forever in eternity.

The Christian life is not determined by a cookie-cutter mold. God calls us all to holiness, but he also gives each of us a *personal vocation*—an invitation to live out our fundamental option in a specific way.

In the next chapter I will describe what a personal vocation is, tell you the story of how I discovered mine, and give some tips that may help you to discover yours.

Questions for Personal Reflection or Discussion

➤ Have I made a fundamental option for holiness? Would anyone know it?

➤ What is my idea of success? Is it the same as God's?

12

Living My Personal Vocation

Before I formed you in the womb I knew you,
before you were born I dedicated you.

—JEREMIAH 1:5

Sometimes I look back on my decision to become a missionary priest and wonder what on earth happened.

I'm the third of seven children. Lawyers run in the family. Priests certainly don't. My parents were traditionally religious, but I don't remember them ever encouraging us to even consider dedicating our lives or careers to religion or the church. But all of us kids knew that the love Mom and Dad had for each other was fed by their individual love affair with God. I breathed in their spirituality as a child, quietly rejected it as passé and cumbersome as an adolescent, and, through some unexpected events, made it my own as a young adult.

I knew Dad would give me only the nominal amount of two thousand dollars when I graduated from high school. It was his way of telling us kids we would need to take personal responsibility for our futures. I knew graduating from high school with a high class ranking and doing well on SATs would be my only money in the bank. If I wanted material success, I would have to get it on my own.

When I met my college roommate, I was intrigued—a California surfer dude who wanted to be a priest! My girlfriend and I used to go on double dates with him and whomever he was dating at the time. I never failed to remind him to let the lucky girl know about his clerical plans. He hemmed and hawed, but it made for great table talk, and it was part of my strategy to spur him on to make up his mind. That year I set Rhett up, so to speak, to talk with priests about a possible vocation and even accompanied him on visits to seminaries. Even though I had nothing personally invested in his decision, I instinctively knew that his decision mattered. One way or the other, it would change people's lives. Looking back now, I see that I reasoned it out in pragmatic terms: Our life is like money. We invest it, and it produces dividends accordingly. If we have only one life, and the consequences are eternal, we'd better make sure the investment is right.

Then I got the bug. *Jonathan, what about you? What are you going to do with your life?* I thought. I didn't hear any voices. There were no apparitions. It was just an interior movement of the soul that grew in intensity over time.

There was nothing about poverty, chastity, or obedience—the vows a missionary priest makes—that excited me. Not my idea of success for sure! And for that very reason I knew the bothersome bug was not of my own creation. Was the growing itch to give up everything, even good and licit things, in order to unite myself more intimately with God a sign of a *vocation?*

152

Clarifying Terms

Before I go on, I should clarify what a *vocation* is. Catholics usually use the word to refer to the pastoral ministry of priests or nuns. Protestants generally don't use the word at all. But the word is biblical, and it involves all of us. *Vocation* comes from the Latin word *vocare*—to call. A vocation is a personal call from God to fulfill a particular mission.

God has in mind for each one of us a unique and nontransferable role within his plan of salvation: "Before I formed you in the womb I knew you, before you were born I dedicated you" (Jer. 1:5).

He communicates this role by calling us to dedicate our life-work and talents to one portion of God's vineyard and to do this in a certain way. Discovering and then *living my personal vocation* is so essential to the Christian life and for finding meaning in suffering that I am proposing it as our second principle of freedom-living.

A vocation usually starts out in very general terms and with time gets more and more specific.

- The first stage of vocational discernment is determining our "state in life." This involves asking God if he is calling us to the married life or to be "single for the Lord," in one or another form, as St. Paul references (1 Cor. 7:32–34).

- If, as in the majority of cases, God is calling us to the married life, the second stage of vocational discernment is selecting a worthy partner (by mutual consent, please!). Romantic attraction is one of the tools God has given us to discern properly his will, but as the divorce rate testifies eloquently, we should also consider other criteria. Hint: good marriage partners help each other get to heaven and work together to bring their children with them.

- The third general stage of vocational discernment is determining where God is calling us to invest our talents. This usually means selecting a profession or career. God calls some to work in education, the business world, the arts, or as a homemaker. Believe it or not, I think God even calls some to work in politics and the media! Our natural talents and deepest desires are generally good indicators of where God is calling us to invest our talents. But we should also keep in mind that sometimes God calls us to give up natural inklings for a greater good.

- God never ceases to call. We can silence his voice in our conscience, but if we take the time to listen, he will always be inviting us to new levels of commitment and union with him. This last stage of vocational discernment is ongoing. It is listening for the Holy Spirit's inspirations, discerning them with prudence and courage, and following them wherever they lead us.

Back to My Story

Mine was an unconventional conflict of interests. I loved business and had already started my own. I loved my girlfriend. I guess I loved God, too, but as icing on my own cake. It wasn't an existential love of God, the type that pervades every aspect of your life. It was a pragmatic one. I knew life would be short, and I preferred to be on the winning side when the whistle was blown.

But I also knew deep down that when it comes to God, existential love is the only sensible type. After all, I couldn't explain how I came to be. Nor could my parents or teachers or biology textbooks give me the whole answer. When I was honest with myself,

I recognized that I, as a person, was fully understandable only in light of a greater being. My hierarchy of values was rather worldly at this point, and it was glaring back at me. If there is a God he should, by definition, be on the top shelf of my life.

Top shelf? What would that look like? Well, if he's personal and cares for me, he made me for a reason, and that reason must be a perfect fit. He also gave me a heart and mind to find out what my purpose might be. That way of thinking got me thinking some more and asking the big question: *God, what do you want me to do for you?*

See how personal the question had become for me? On account of no merit of my own, the living presence of God had seeped beyond the crusty surface of my ambitions. My idea of success was beginning to change. Making money was still a good thing. A desire for human love, too—of a woman and of a future family of my own. The attraction to power and influence did not vanish. I hadn't lost the natural gusto for any of these.

Their relative importance is what began to change. If Jesus is God, then he's trustworthy. If he asks me to do this or that, or anything else, it's because it will be a perfect fit. I know him and I trust him.

Having dragged my roommate to more than one seminary, I had scoped out the lay of the land of priestdom. As in any grouping of humanity, there was a little bit of everything in the men he and I met: weakness and strength. But the ones who caught my attention were the happy ones. They had made what for me seemed like the ultimate choice of selflessness, and still they smiled. Initially, I wondered what had possessed them to give up so much for such paltry return. So I asked them. No, I grilled them. I was determined to find out what made them different from me, hoping to discover some anomaly to put my heart at ease. Their stories were amazingly different one from another, but they were stitched together by a single thread. They had received an invitation from God to live for others with an undivided heart.

And as I listened to their personal narratives, my desperation grew. The voice speaking to my soul was clear and kind: "And, Jonathan, why not you?" Well, for lots of reasons! I named them off to God, but mostly to myself. Why would he give me desires for so many good things only to ask me to give them up? Those desires, after all, were absolutely natural, wired into me by my maker. But quite honestly, I didn't want answers to my quandary. I preferred escape routes. And I found them: more entrepreneurial enterprise, more cold beers on Friday nights with the guys, and, yes, my girlfriend. Good things.

But with every new activity, the question of fullness and perfection remained. What was I made for? Silently, cautiously, I had already assented to the only question that matters: "If I were to know what God wanted from me, would I be willing to do it, no matter the cost?" The water was coming to a boil. The question persisted: "Jonathan, why not you?"

Maybe the question seems absurd. There are lots of ways to live for others. Being a good dad and husband and a productive citizen is no small task. I can't give a scientific explanation for the movement of my young heart to this type of total service. The radical nature of it stirred in me nobility I never knew I had. I wanted to live with an undivided heart given to others out of love for God. I also knew the idea wasn't mine. If I believed in a clockwork God, there would be no real explanation for such conflicting desires. But I had personally experienced, in prayer, in the sacraments, and in creation, a providential God who cared about me and intervened in human history. I didn't have all the answers, but I knew he did. If it was he who was doing the calling, my trust was not in vain.

Running parallel to my quest to know God's will for me was the issue of eternity. Life is short. Eternity isn't. We have only one chance to get it right. The calculation didn't include fear or guilt, or at least I don't think so. I hope it was practical faith. If God exists, his Word is true. He says this life is preparation for the next. The best preparation is to do his will. I don't want to settle for anything less.

That summer my roommate, Rhett, would make his move. He was to spend the summer in Connecticut at a "discernment program," a trial run of sorts. Between travels with my little business, I decided to visit him and make sure everything was OK. And the tables turned: Rhett left, and I stayed.

I remember the moment I decided to sign up for good. Lots of tears, then lasting peace and joy. I had some explaining to do—to family, friends, and *the* friend. When I broke the news to her, there were more tears but, in the moment, less peace and no joy. We both hurt. I explained this to her the only way I knew how: "I think the invitation is coming from God . . . and he knows about you. That means he's got a better plan for you than me [*not hard to imagine!*], and so I had better get out of the way." God had invited me to set aside natural desires for supernatural ones. There were no strings attached, no divine threats or ultimatums. He had left the choice up to me, and he promised me he would stay with me, close by my side, no matter which way I went. I could stay or I could leave, freely.

And so could have the saints of old! I thought of Abraham, who set off for a land unknown; Moses, who led the chosen people. I knew Saul had become Paul. Theresa of Calcutta fed the poor. Billy Graham and John Paul II preached to the masses. And each of their decisions mattered. I wouldn't dare compare my decision with any of theirs, but I knew that, on a very different scale, it was really the same thing.

Mom and Dad were shocked but fully supportive. I knew they would be. That's the way they lived: "Never say no to the invites of

God." Next on my shock list was my roommate Rhett. "You've got to watch out for her, man," I told him, referring to my girlfriend. He promised me he would. And he did: Rhett and Tosha are now married with five children, and we remain close friends.

Vocation and Holiness

I know that many of you live more nobly and heroically in your own vocations than I could ever hope to live in mine. Being a mom or a dad, a husband or a wife, loyal employee, and an enterprising contributor to society and to Christian culture is no small task.

I've chosen *living my personal vocation* as the second principle for freedom-living because it is the first way to make practical our fundamental option for holiness. Our vocation and the responsibilities that come with it serve as a framework for our spiritual life. If you are married with children, God is probably not calling you to go off on your own for a year to serve AIDS victims in Africa. It would seem a very good and noble thing to do, but it would not be a *holy* thing to do. It would conflict with the duties of your vocation.

We have already described holiness as union with God and have said that the ordinary way we collaborate with his work of sanctification is through submitting our will to his. If God doesn't want me to go to Africa; if he doesn't want me to priest or a pastor; if he isn't asking me to sell my beach house or motorboat—doing any of that is not being holy, because none of it is his will. The opposite is also true: Am I willing to sell my motorboat?

The Pharisees were the experts in the fulfillment of "the law" in the days of Jesus. At face value, they were the "holy" ones because they knew all of the right things to do and say and they carried out "God's will" with perfection.

But Jesus wasn't so happy with them. Why not? In the eighteenth chapter of Luke's Gospel we find out. It is the parable of the Pharisee and the Publican. Both of them go to the temple to pray. The Pharisee goes to the front and begins to talk to God. His prayer consists in listing off all of his own wonderful religious qualities and holy acts. He is full of himself. The Publican, on the other hand, stays in the back and hides his face. He beats his breast with shame and guilt. His prayer is primarily a petition for God's mercy. Jesus ends the story by saying the Publican went back to his home justified before God and the Pharisee did not.

So, like the Pharisees, we can think we are serving God and working for holiness when in fact we are just full of ourselves. Here are a few questions we can ask when we are not sure what God's will is in any given situation. They will help us stay objective in the living of our personal vocation.

1. What does Scripture have to say about my decision?

2. Has the Church offered wisdom about the issue?

3. Does this opportunity come into conflict with any known duties of my state in life (marriage, family, job, and so forth)?

4. Have I consulted a holy and prudent man or woman of God?

5. Am I giving weight to selfish motives, even unconsciously?

6. What would I suggest to someone else in the same situation?

Living my personal vocation is linked intimately to making sense of suffering. Everything in our lives—with the exception of our own evildoing—is part of God's perfect plan. But when this plan comes in the form of suffering, it's not so easy to recognize. When we are living our vocation to the maximum, we know we are at the center of God's will. It is from this position that we can best see suffering for what it is. It is not coincidence or bad luck. It is not fate or bad karma. It is God offering us the most privileged path to holiness: a sharing of his own cross.

Questions for Personal Reflection or Discussion

> ➤ Have I asked the question "God, what do you want me to do for you?" Has he responded?

> ➤ Have I accepted suffering as part of God's plan for my life?

13

Uniting My Suffering to His, for Others

*Now I rejoice in my sufferings for your sake, and in
my flesh I am filling up what is lacking in the afflictions of
Christ on behalf of his body, which is the church.*

—COLOSSIANS 1:24

If you are suffering deeply, until now perhaps you have seen the promise of a "greater good" as an object of blind faith at best. More likely, you have seen it as philosophical gibberish. That is because it would seem that any decent response from God to human suffering would have something to do with improving the present, not only the future. You may be asking, "If I am the one who is suffering and I'm suffering now, where is the greater good for me? And if it's coming, why does God make me wait?"

In this chapter I propose a third principle for freedom-living, one that has the potential to change your life right now. I don't say that lightly; it is the first time I hint at quick fixes in this book. I say it with confidence because I have seen God's grace transform so many lives from one day to the next when they learn to live by this principle.

We easily complain that God doesn't respond to human suffering with a promise to make it go away. But his promise includes something better: "I will make your suffering beautiful and purposeful like mine."

The cross of Jesus—in all of its bloody horror—should be tragic, but because it redeems, it is holy. It should be sad, but it is our joy. Every drop of his blood is precious. Every bead of his sweat is love. Ours can be, too.

The quote at the beginning of this chapter from the apostle Paul reveals a new vision of suffering: *human suffering has real power and real purpose.*

Real Power

In the suffering and death of Jesus, God unites himself in a special way to those who suffer. He wants to be close to the afflicted. He wants his wounds of love to heal our wounds of rebellion. Of course, as is his way, before working this miracle he waits on us. He doesn't push. He desires for us to second his initial act of love.

We can unite our suffering to Christ's suffering with a simple lifting of the heart: "Jesus, I offer this suffering up to you, out of love for you." Real power comes forth. Try it.

Jesus promises strength, peace, and ultimate victory for those who unite their tribulations to his: "I have told you this so that you might have peace in me. In the world you will have trouble, but take courage, I have conquered the world" (John 16:33).

The power of uniting our suffering to his is not psychological;

it is redemptive. It flows from what we can call the *creative character of Christian suffering.* Jesus' sufferings brought forth—or *created*—the redemption of mankind. When we unite our sufferings to his, we, too, partake in this creative nature as members of the Body of Christ. We are not redeemers. We are not healers. But inasmuch as we become sharers of Christ's suffering, in our own very human way we complete the suffering through which God redeemed the world.

Nobody has said it better than the Apostle Paul: " . . . and in my flesh I am filling up what is lacking in the afflictions of Christ on behalf of his body, which is the church" (Col. 1:24).

But I thought Christ's redemption was once and for all. When Pope John Paul II, the great suffering pope who stayed in the public eye up to the very end because he believed in the value of Christian suffering, reflected on Paul's words, he asked and then answered that same question in his apostolic letter *Salvifici Doloris:*

> *Does this mean that the Redemption achieved by Christ is not complete? No. It only means that the Redemption, accomplished through satisfactory love, remains always open to all love expressed in human suffering. In this dimension—the dimension of love—the Redemption, which has already been completely accomplished, is, in a certain sense, constantly being accomplished. Christ achieved the Redemption completely and to the very limits, but at the same time he did not bring it to a close. In this redemptive suffering, through which the Redemption of the world was accomplished, Christ opened himself from the beginning to every human suffering and constantly does so.*

This idea of sharing in the redemptive work of God *through suffering* may be new to many of us, but it shouldn't come as a surprise. I am sure you can see how perfectly it meshes with what we have until now called *the pedagogy of God*. God loves to involve us in his divine work. He turns spectators into players. This is his idea of Church.

Real Purpose

It is only because of Church—the mystical body of Christ—that we can really speak of completing "what is lacking" in Christ's suffering. We continue the work of Christ's redemptive work on earth, as Paul says, "on behalf of his body, which is the church."

If our suffering united to Christ's suffering carries power, then its purpose is the building up of the body of Christ. In the most real of senses, the supernatural one, we can now say we never suffer alone, and, most important, we never suffer uselessly. Even if nobody else knows we are in pain, we can offer it up for the good of others. And we can be comforted in knowing that someone, someplace, is offering up his suffering for us. Our relationship as a human family, and more particularly as members of the Christian body, is the interconnected playing field of God's grace.

I suggested earlier that you tap into the power of redemptive suffering with the words "Jesus, I offer this suffering up to you, out of love for you." Let me now add a few words to this prayer. They express purpose:

"Jesus, I offer this suffering up to you, out of love for you, and for the sake of _____, a member of your Church."

When we pray through our suffering, we imitate and participate in the most powerful prayers of Jesus. Think of the Garden of Gethsemane: "If you are willing, take this cup away from me; still, not my will but yours be done" (Luke 22:42). How different

Jesus' prayer of suffering was from the attitude of the apostles. He begged Peter, James, and John to stay up with him and to "pray that you may not undergo the test" (Luke 22:43), but they failed him miserably. Jesus found them sleeping "from grief," says the Gospel of Luke (22:45). The disciples had not yet learned what to do with their grief. They didn't understand the power or the purpose of human suffering united to their master's. In the face of such meaningless internal turmoil, the apostles decided that sleep—unconsciousness—was the best alternative. The disciples were slow learners, like most of us.

Christian Suffering as a Path to Joy

I know a woman named Sarah who has endured much more than her fair share of trauma. It seems the more good she tries to do, the more bad luck she has. Moved by high ideals, she took a job as a high school principal in a low-income neighborhood. Her long suffering began when a fight broke out between a Hispanic student and a black student. When she stepped in to break it up, they both turned on her. They jumped on her legs and back so hard and for so long that they left her semiparalyzed for life. After many operations and long hospital stays, Sarah was finally able to get around on her own in a wheelchair. Determined to make the best of her situation, she moved to Italy for graduate studies, where I eventually met her.

Her stay in Italy has been marked by one tragedy after another. I've never seen anything like it. Her misadventures have included falling in the bathroom and fracturing her neck, being mugged and beaten by a man on the street, and most recently, being hit by a car in her wheelchair as she was checking her apartment mailbox.

A letter from her that I received at Christmas fills in the rest of her harrowing story. She is explaining why she hasn't been in touch over the last few months:

"In a nutshell, since I last wrote, I have been in and out of Careggi Hospital in Florence, only to be finally rejected from their research program. On top of that, I lost the function of my intestines; was denied my Social Security disability income for several months (thought it was resolved but it's not); had my neuro-urological surgery postponed until I lose sixty to eighty pounds (in five months, I have lost six pounds using a supervised diet); dropped, broke and lost most of my contact numbers in my cell phone as they were not on my SIM card; lost another year of study at the university (this means I may lose my legal permission to stay in Italy); had my rent increased; stress-fractured my jaw due to clenching my teeth from the pain I endure when my urine backs into my kidney; had my Dell Notebook of ten years "crash and die"; and just learned that my mother has metastasized small-cell lung cancer."

If I didn't know Sarah personally, I would wonder if the letter weren't a tad exaggerated. It's not. Just picturing her story could serve the good purpose of putting our own sufferings into perspective. But the real lesson she has taught me is the beauty of redemptive suffering. This may be hard to believe, but I promise you Sarah is a very joyful person! She reveals her secret to happiness in a very simple way in the following paragraphs, extracted from the same letter:

"I can tell you from my own lived experience of these past months that keeping my eyes fixed on Jesus on the Cross gets me through the day. I now know that to ask 'why' is very, very stupid! It accomplishes nothing but agitation that disturbs the soul and wastes time that I can use for the intentions and needs of others. That list is endless, and that list is what needs my attention, my sacrifices, my sufferings, my energy. So, I can really say to you that

that simple prayer we learned as children, 'The Morning Offering,' in its profundity, is really my compass to filling up what is lacking in the sufferings of Christ.

"For most of my life, I really wrestled with Thomas Aquinas's 'In His Will, is our peace.' But I must tell you, he was so right on the mark. Please do keep me and my family in your prayers, as I will you, that we ALL come to know, love, and serve God by living this truth of our faith. It really does keep 'the worries' away. God bless you. Please forgive me if I caused you any annoyance by not writing sooner."

Sarah is a special soul, but even so I don't think the way she has approached her suffering and its joyful results are out of our reach. It is Jesus' way, and he promised to be our way, truth, and life. Sarah found what the apostle Paul found: "I *rejoice* in my sufferings for your sake." Joy can be found in the midst of suffering by overcoming the sense of suffering's uselessness.

Christian Suffering as a Path to Holiness

Down through the centuries we can see a pattern of personal holiness worked out in the crucible of suffering. If, as we have said previously, suffering can make us more human—more realistic and appreciative of life, more understanding of others and more sensible to their pain—then we can similarly say *Christian* suffering makes us more divine. Through it we become more sensitive to and integrated with the things of God.

I saw this happen this past week. A Brazilian priest came to Rome to study for his doctorate. After not showing up for several activities, one of his housemates went to his room and found him unconscious in bed. He was rushed to the hospital and spent the next two weeks in a coma and in intensive care. None of the dozens of tests he underwent pointed to a sure cause. Eventually the doctors diagnosed his strokelike symptoms as the result of a rare virus in the brain.

After fifty-two days in the hospital, Father Orivaldo returned to the college a changed man. He walked slowly, but he was going to be OK. I was in the church when Father Orivaldo presided at his first mass since falling ill. There were just two of us present, and this grown man cried through the entire service. Later that day, Father Orivaldo told me that although he had been a minister for many years, he considered this to have been his first mass. "I was closer to God today in this Eucharistic celebration than I have ever been before," he told me. Through suffering he discovered a new dimension of his life and vocation. Through God's grace he is now on the road to true interior maturity and spiritual greatness.

In chapter 7 I began to tell you about Marcela and her long fight with MS. I promised to come back to her story. This section on suffering as a path to holiness is the place to take up where we left off. Marcela knew I was writing this book, and she agreed to record a long and very personal conversation about her saga, including the good times and bad, the ups and downs, hopes and dashed hopes that come with chronic illness. Our conversation took place just days before she was to head out of the country to undergo a new trial treatment that would include almost one month of solitary confinement. She was calm, but also very realistic about what this would mean. "Yes, I'm scared," she said more than once, "but I'm peaceful."

Pushing the envelope a bit, I asked her to stop giving me answers based on faith: "Marcela, it's great that you can talk about uniting your suffering to God, and all the hope you have in heaven, but not everyone has such faith. Surely there has got to be something they can do to deal with their suffering and find the kind of peace you have."

"Father Jonathan," she said, "I would love to be able to give some technique that could really help, but there is none. If I did not have a relationship with God, and know his love for me, and his perfect plan, my suffering would be unbearable. I just don't see any light whatsoever."

And Marcela walks the walk. It's not all pretty words. I told you she is a vocalist. Here is a song she wrote from her bed. I still get goose bumps when I hear it for the umpteenth time, but I want you at least to see the words. This is not theory. It is love, tried and proven in the crucible of redemptive suffering.

I CAN LOVE YOU JUST THE SAME

From my bed and in pajamas, I can love you just the same. . .
From my bed and in pajamas, if this is your will. . .
In this way too, you are here with me, as if trying to say. . .
That in straw and swaddling clothes, you too loved me. . .
Unable even to take care of myself, I can love you just the
*   same. . .*
Unable even to take care of myself, if this is your will. . .
In this way too you are here with me, as if trying to say. . .
That when your mother carried you in your arms, you too
*   loved me. . .*
Even with so few accomplishments, I can love you just the
*   same.*
Even with so few accomplishments, if this is your will. . .
You have already walked this path, the one I want to follow. . .
In a little town, for thirty years, you too loved me. . .
In my fear and bathed here in tears, I can love you just the
*   same. . .*
In my fear and bathed here in tears, if this is your will. . .
You have already walked this path, the one I want to follow. . .
With loud cries, and sweat like drops of blood, you
*   loved me. . .*

So weak and useless, I can love you just the same. . .
So weak and useless, if this is your will. . .
You have already walked this path, the one I want to follow. . .
Immobilized, from the cross, you loved me. . .
No matter what happens . . . I can love you just the same. . .
No matter what happens . . . , this will be your will!
You will not leave me alone, you will be right here,
Because from all eternity, you loved me.
You will not leave me alone, you will be right here,
Because from all eternity, you loved me.

For every one of these beautiful stories, I could tell you many others that are far less inspiring. That's because suffering on its own does not draw us to God; it just raises the stakes on life and on accepting or rejecting God's grace. Either we can sulk in self-pity and slowly whither away or we can participate in a wonderful interchange of wills where the one who is suffering unites his will to God's. The transformation of suffering into a purposeful act of love can be done only in the heart of the one who suffers.

This is the "taking up" of one's cross about which Jesus spoke: "Whoever wishes to come after me must deny himself, take up his cross, and follow me" (Matt. 16:24). And on another occasion: "I say to you, unless a grain of wheat falls to the ground and dies, it remains just a grain of wheat; but if it dies, it produces much fruit" (John 12:24).

There is no real Gospel without the cross. The Sermon on the Mount is one of the most universally loved passages in the Bible, but I think it is also one of the most misunderstood. Most people quote it as the discourse of divine love, the laying out of God's social agenda, so to speak, including his preferential love for the poor—and it certainly is all of that. But there is much more to it. When we look at this passage from the point of view of suffering, we see that God's promise is tied to the holiness of life. Jesus is not saying only "Blessed are those who suffer," but rather "Blessed are those who suffer and respond to that suffering with virtue and love." Here it is:

> *Blessed are the poor in spirit, for theirs is the kingdom of heaven.*
> *Blessed are those who mourn, for they will be comforted.*
> *Blessed are the meek, for they will inherit the land.*
> *Blessed are those who hunger and thirst for righteousness, for they will be satisfied.*
> *Blessed are the merciful, for they will be shown mercy.*
> *Blessed are the clean of heart, for they will see God.*
> *Blessed are the peacemakers, for they will be called children of God.*
> *Blessed are they who are persecuted for the sake of righteousness, for theirs is the kingdom of heaven.*
> *Blessed are you when they insult you and persecute you and utter every kind of evil against you falsely because of me.*
> *Rejoice and be glad, for your reward will be great in heaven. Thus they persecuted the prophets who were before you.*
> *(Matt. 5:3–12)*

Questions for Personal Reflection or Discussion

➤ Do I understand why my suffering has value in the eyes of God?

➤ Am I willing to take part in God's Promise and offer up my suffering for the sake of others?

14

Being the Hands and Feet of Christ

As you go, make this proclamation, "The kingdom of heaven is at hand." Cure the sick, raise the dead, cleanse lepers, drive out demons. Without cost you have received; without cost you are to give.

—MATTHEW 10:7–8

The passage above from the Gospel of Matthew is the spiritual foundation for our fourth principle for freedom-living. Jesus sends us out to be his hands and feet in a world of great hurt.

I always imagined the lifestyle of an international journalist to be exhilarating and personally rewarding, but soon after I started going out on the big news stories to offer social and ethical commentary, I realized it's not always so romantic. One of the most painful parts of journalism is encountering local suffering up close, getting to know good people and their very complicated problems only to have to pack up one's gear and move on a few days later.

In February 2006 I went to Venezuela to cover a massive march in honor of the country's religious traditions. I could talk at length about the trip and what I learned about the religious, political, and social landscape of this great nation, but there is one story from those days that is of particular relevance to this book and this chapter. Rosa's story illustrates how social factors can sap people of spiritual energy and make people's finding sense in suffering all but impossible on their own. It also points to God's response to this human predicament, an invitation to live our fourth principle for freedom-living.

My cameraman, Alfredo, and I were getting some shots of the National Assembly—a stately building in pristine condition that houses Venezuela's legislative body. Soldiers patrolled the property. I won't easily forget the brisk military exercises that were taking place up and down the street. Unsure of how well my clerical presence would be received in this part of the city, I tried to keep a low profile and let Alfredo do his thing.

I crossed the street and ducked under the cover of a low awning in order to get some relief from the hot sun. As I turned my head, I saw light coming through a cavity in the tall concrete wall against which I was leaning. A rusty, decrepit door—of sorts—hung partly open, a chain and padlock swinging from its midsection. I peeped in and then heard an angry shout: "¡Qué quieres?!" (*What do you want?!*) It was a woman in her midforties. I stepped in to excuse myself for having been so nosy, and at the same time to get a better look.

"I'm sorry, ma'am, I was just passing by and was curious." As I looked at her, I couldn't help but notice the scene taking place behind her back. There were kids everywhere—barefoot, shabbily dressed, and very dirty. *Is this a home?* I thought to myself. It looked more like an abandoned construction site.

It was a home. An extended family of more than twenty people claimed residence in this ramshackle lot. Cardboard served as both bed and roof. It was a weekday, and these kids were not in school. The young adults looked like they were up to no good, on edge and angry. When Rosa saw my collar, she relaxed a bit. She waved me into the lot, and the gate shut behind me. After a few minutes of chitchatting she told me all of her woes, and they were many. She didn't ask me for a dime. She just wanted someone to lend her an attentive ear.

The most shocking part of her personal story was not the level of poverty (I've seen it in many places) or even the fact that this poverty took shape directly across the street from a symbol of a very wealthy government (in Washington, D. C., this happens too). Rather, it was her fierce and absolute trust that the government was going to pull her out of her poverty at any moment. The family had been in this hellhole for over nine years, and still she was waiting. I pressed for motives with questions like these: "If the government building is right across the street, why do you think they haven't helped you yet? Do you expect a turn for the good anytime soon?"

Sadly, she didn't have a lot of answers, but she was sure of one thing: at any moment, a government official was going to cross that street and hand her keys to a brand-new home and lots of other good things.

Perhaps Rosa will eventually receive aid. I don't know. I do know it hasn't happened in all of these years, despite many promises that it would. It is sad to think that Rosa's only hope is looking ahead to relief that may never come. She has built her life around a fairy-tale ending. With such great trust in a political savior, she has no motivation to invest in the future; why send the kids to school, learn a trade, or even clean up the house? She prefers to wait. Or more likely, maybe that's all she knows how to do.

Rosa's story made a big impact on me because I knew she was stuck in a rut. In some ways I could understand her passivity; she didn't know anything else. Unless someone were to come and teach her how to build a life for herself and her family, she would continue in her flaccid misery.

She needed help, yes, but not *only* from the government. She needed a neighbor, a Good Samaritan.

The next day on the way to the Caracas airport, we passed by thousands of "homes" in no better shape than Rosa's. I looked out the tinted windows of the jeep and tried to make small talk with my crew about less somber things. But how could we talk about anything else? We were engulfed in material and moral desolation. The one-room shacks were shabbily built one on top of the other along the steep mountain slopes. The faces of the toddlers and small children were dirty, grim, and, for the moment, still quite innocent. Their older brothers and sisters looked just as poor, but more jaded and streetwise.

Who would help these folks? We had done our thing, and we were on our way home.

The emptiness and sadness we feel when we look at other people's pains and can do nothing about them is a healthy feeling. It is God's way of reminding us that his master plan for dealing with human suffering includes us. We were made to live for others, to be balm for their wounds. We were made to be God's hands and feet on earth. When we see people abandoned by society, it means God's plan has been frustrated by selfishness and sin.

So what should we do?

The Good Samaritan

The parable of the Good Samaritan is, hands down, my favorite Gospel passage (Luke 10:25–37). It is Jesus telling us what he would like to *do* with our suffering and what we can *do* with the suffering of others on his behalf—good Samaritans imitating the Good Samaritan. It is the perfect synthesis of our fourth principle for freedom living: being the hands and feet of Christ.

You probably remember the story. Three voyagers were making the trek from Jerusalem to Jericho. One was a priest, the other a Levite, and the third a Samaritan. When the priest and Levite came upon the unsightly scene of a man badly beaten and left for dead on the side of the road, they crossed to the other side and went their merry way. They had more important things to do. The Samaritan was on the same road, but he "was moved with compassion at the sight." The Latin etymology of the word *compassion* is "to suffer with." The Samaritan went over to the victim and bound up his wounds. He then "took him to an inn and cared for him." He entrusted the convalescing man to the continued care of an innkeeper and promised to pay for any expenses upon his return.

Jesus uses the priest and Levite as prototypes of the religious elite who lose sight of God—the real object of religion—and become infected with impure motives. By cultural heritage these men were upright and prepared to do the right thing. They knew the law and honored their family traditions. The Samaritan, on the other hand, is Jesus' prototype of the social outcast who, nonetheless, has a naturally pure and good heart. By cultural heritage he was considered a religious outsider and would have every right to plead spiritual ignorance. But by *choice,* he was a man after the heart of God: he responded to the passive suffering of others by tending to their needs.

In Jesus' narration, it was the Samaritan, not the priest or the Levite, who understood the second greatest commandment: "Love your neighbor as yourself."

What a lesson Jesus gave us! The Samaritan is the real deal; he's Christianity in action. Last chapter's principle for freedom-living—

uniting our suffering to Christ's suffering and offering it up for the sake of others—leads us gently into the bigger context of active love of neighbor. God didn't save us from our sins in a passive way. He *came* to earth. He *acted*. If God's pedagogy is to involve us in his redemptive work, is it any wonder his promise to bring a greater good out of our suffering is tied to *our action, in his name?* When we live charity and love of neighbor, we are taking part in his strategy to heal life's hurts.

The decision of the Samaritan to tend to this poor man's suffering flows out of genuine love for the downtrodden. He sees him lying in the street, goes over to him, takes him in his arms, tends to his wounds, brings him to a shelter, finds a long-term caregiver, and even pays for his extended care. The Good Samaritan is Jesus showing us the movements of his own hands and feet. He is saying, "This is how I want to care of you, and how you are called to care for your neighbor, on my behalf."

I love this parable because I think it reveals the heart of God in a very special way. It is as if Jesus were explaining to us the priorities of his Father in heaven and how he put them into action on earth. Have you ever wondered why Jesus spent so much of his short public ministry healing the sick? He had only three years to preach his message and establish his Church. If I had been given the task of putting together a business plan for him to accomplish these goals, I probably would have told him to dedicate his time to big crowds and public discourses. Instead, Jesus visited individual homes and concerned himself with social outcasts. He touched and healed lepers and rubbed mud on the eyes of the blind. He brought back to life one widow's son . . . because he felt compassion for her. He raised Lazarus from the dead. . . . because he was his friend. Jesus, the son of God, works one-on-one, and he uses the human touch.

The Scripture says Jesus went around "doing good" (Acts 10:38). "Doing good," in this sense, means Jesus responded to physical and spiritual suffering by curing people of their ailments. When he points to the Good Samaritan as a model, he is in fact pointing to himself and then back at us. Jesus is saying we can be his hands and feet. We can continue his mission of bringing comfort and healing to the poor.

So essential to Jesus' teaching is our fourth principle of freedom-living that, according to the Scriptures, it will be God's measuring stick on the Day of Judgment. Have you ever wondered what God will say to you when you meet him face to face at the hour of your death? I think about it often, and I try to recall one passage in particular. There is only one place in the Bible that specifically describes what the Final Judgment will be like. It is in the Gospel of Matthew. Read these verses slowly, and let them sink in. It is Jesus telling us what is going to be on life's final exam. I think it is the best explanation of this fourth principle of freedom-living: being the hands and feet of Christ.

> *When the Son of Man comes in his glory, and all the angels*
> *with him, he will sit upon his glorious throne,*
> *and all the nations will be assembled before him. And*
> *he will separate them one from another, as a shepherd*
> *separates the sheep from the goats.*
> *He will place the sheep on his right and the goats on*
> *his left.*
> *Then the king will say to those on his right, "Come, you*
> *who are blessed by my Father. Inherit the kingdom*
> *prepared for you from the foundation of the world.*
> *For I was hungry and you gave me food, I was thirsty and*
> *you gave me drink, a stranger and you welcomed me,*

*naked and you clothed me, ill and you cared for me, in prison
and you visited me."*

*Then the righteous will answer him and say, "Lord, when did
we see you hungry and feed you, or thirsty and give you
drink?*

*When did we see you a stranger and welcome you, or naked
and clothe you?*

When did we see you ill or in prison, and visit you?"

*And the king will say to them in reply, "Amen, I say to you,
whatever you did for one of these least brothers of mine,
you did for me."*

*Then he will say to those on his left, "Depart from me, you
accursed, into the eternal fire prepared for the devil and
his angels.*

*For I was hungry and you gave me no food, I was thirsty and
you gave me no drink,*

*a stranger and you gave me no welcome, naked and you
gave me no clothing, ill and in prison, and you did not
care for me."*

*Then they will answer and say, "Lord, when did we see you
hungry or thirsty or a stranger or naked or ill or in prison,
and not minister to your needs?"*

*He will answer them, "Amen, I say to you, what you did not
do for one of these least ones, you did not do for me."*

*And these will go off to eternal punishment, but the righteous
to eternal life. (Matt. 25:31–46)*

Besides being a good and stiff warning, this passage also reveals
more truth about God's purpose and plan for suffering in general.
Not only can our suffering serve as an instrument of personal sanctification, as we explained in the last chapter; it can also release
love in the hearts of those who are witnesses to the suffering of

others. The suffering of our neighbor is an invitation to get in the game of creating, to be a player in the project of building a civilization of love. Imagine a world where nobody ever hurt, where all was bliss, where there were no tears or tiredness, no dread or disappointment. Wouldn't we be tempted to live a completely self-centered existence? Living this fourth principle of freedom-living is not only about bringing relief to others; it is about filling out God's plan for our own sanctification. Being the hands and feet of Christ does as much good for the Good Samaritan as it does for the victim he cures.

What Kind of Good Samaritan Should I Be?

When I boarded a plane in Caracas and went home to relative luxury, was I doing the right thing? Or was I crossing the road with the priest and Levite because I had more important things to do?

As human beings we are limited in every way: we can be in only one place at a time, our time and resources run out quickly, and we get old and die. How do we decide, then, how to be the Good Samaritan within our physical and emotional limits? My heart was captivated by the poor in Venezuela, but if I were to go to any other country on that continent, I know I could find cases of like misery, and my heart, I hope, would be drawn there, too. What kind of Good Samaritan should I be?

We can answer this question, related to the one that will be on life's final exam, only by bringing together the four principles of freedom-living that we have seen. Here they are again:

- Making a fundamental option for holiness

- Living your personal vocation

- Uniting your suffering to his, for the sake of others

- Being the hands and feet of Christ

God's principles never contradict one another. Each of these principles depends on and builds upon the previous ones. Our fundamental option for holiness, for example, is made concrete through discovering and living our personal vocation, including all the obligations that flow from it. Life circumstances make that vocation clearer with the passing of time. Sometimes those circumstances include the suffering of being laid up in bed with serious illness or struggling to keep a marriage together. In all of this we can find holiness and be faithful to our vocations by uniting our suffering to Jesus. It is in this big-picture look at God's will for us, moving from one principle to the next, that we can discern how we are called to be Christ's hands and feet for others.

In explaining how to discern one's personal vocation, I mentioned the need to take into consideration the duties of our state in life. I knew God wasn't calling me to stay in Venezuela, because I had other duties that were directly linked to my vocation that would be impossible to fulfill otherwise. If you are married and have children, God is not calling you to abandon them in order to work in an orphanage in Mozambique. (You would be creating more orphans!) But our many duties don't get us off the hook from being the hands and feet of Christ. The parable of the Good Samaritan and the description of the Final Judgment tell us that we can be sure we have not heard well God's voice if we think our vocation is to live only or evenly primarily for ourselves. The priest and the Levite were probably on their way to do good things. Maybe they would even have helped this poor man if they had been any less busy. Their busyness, though, was their own. It was not the will, or the business, of God.

Jesus is saying the sick, the lonely, the dying, the incarcerated, the unclothed, the depressed, and the poor in general must be a *priority* in our lives. Proactive charity is not optional in the Christian life.

Where Do I Begin?

The old saying "Charity begins at home" contains a lot of wisdom. If you are feeding the poor at a homeless shelter every weekend yet haven't spent a full day with the kids in months, something is wrong. The first "poor" we are called to serve are those that are around us every day. But we must keep in mind that there are different types of poverty. We can be spiritually poor, emotionally poor, or physically poor. If God put our husband, wife, children, relatives, business partners, coworkers, friends, and even the local gas-station attendant in our lives, we can assume he wants us to reach out to their areas of "poverty" in some way. Being the hands and feet of Christ in relation to a store clerk, gas-station attendant, or other casual acquaintance, for example, may simply mean going beyond the usual formalities of "Good morning" and "Have a nice day" and asking him about his family or how he spent the holidays. It doesn't take much. It is having the courage to enter people's lives and suffering in an appropriate and Christ-like way.

Charity begins at home, but it can't end there. We are called to make a positive difference in the world and in the Church. And we can't say we are just too busy.

There are a million ways to get involved and change society for the better. The important thing is that we do it like Christ, meaning our action should flow out of a genuine love for mankind and a desire to build up the Kingdom of God on earth. Otherwise, we are just being social workers: we will do good work, but we won't be imitating Jesus. Jesus healed the sick and fed the hungry, but he also forgave sins, and the first made no sense without the second. He was interested in the whole person and, most important, that person's eternal salvation. If we want to be the hands and feet of Christ, we must focus on the internal conversion of our own hearts so that the work we do is truly an extension of Jesus' redemptive mission. In order to be Christ's presence on earth, we must learn to see with his eyes, and our hearts must learn to beat in unison with his.

The following are a few simple ideas for how to begin to see and judge the world and our many relationships with the eyes and heart of God. If you put these ideas into practice, I think the fourth principle of freedom-living will become a part of who you are. These suggestions won't make the decisions for you—where to invest your time, what "poor" you are called to serve, how to make a hierarchy among your many responsibilities that corresponds to godly priorities—but they will tune you in to hearing the voice of God. They will sensitize your heart to know how you can make a difference in this world that suffers.

The four ideas that follow are facets of the same virtue: *charity*. It is the essence of the heart of Jesus and the unmistakable sign of the Christian.

Form the Habit of Speaking Well of Others

You may be surprised that I put "speaking well of others" at the top of my list. Is that even a virtue? What about speaking the truth? The two are very rarely in conflict, in fact. We often lean on the excuse of "speaking our mind" or "just being honest" to placate our conscience when we are in fact talking negatively of other people in order to gratify our own ego. I am not suggesting we become experts in polite talk or political correctness. That comes and goes and leaves no mark. I mean regularly making a concerted effort to build up in the eyes of others the good reputation of our friends, coworkers, neighbors, family members, and, yes, even our enemies.

Certainly there are occasions when, on account of position or responsibility, we must give a negative assessment of someone. But even when we do this, we can do it in a way that gives the benefit of the doubt to the person in question and doesn't go beyond facts into character assassination or even useless speculation.

If you take up the habit of speaking well of people, especially when they themselves are not present, your heart will soon follow the beauty of your words. You will judge people with the patience and purity of God. The book of James is a great place to go to know what God's Word says about the importance of controlling our language.

> *If anyone does not fall short in speech, he is a perfect man,*
>   *able to bridle his whole body also. . . .*
> *It is the same with ships: even though they are so large and*
>   *driven by fierce winds, they are steered by a very small*
>   *rudder wherever the pilot's inclination wishes.*
> *In the same way the tongue is a small member and yet has*
>   *great pretensions.* (James 3:2–5)

I spoke this morning with a friend of mine, Jim, who is starting a new business. He had been having difficulty working with his new business partner. Both have been self-employed for a long time, and now, all of a sudden, in their new venture they have to float their equally brilliant ideas past each other before acting.

Jim called to tell me about a big breakthrough in the difficulty. About three weeks ago he and his wife, Stephanie, were lying in bed late at night lamenting to one another all the annoying things the other business partner does. As they were trying to fall asleep they recalled point by point how the personality and work style of this man was driving them both crazy. At some point in their late-night conversation, Stephanie realized that instead of consoling one another or coming up with solutions, they were making the problem worse. They let it rest and decided to talk about it in the morning.

This couple, I should note, are among the nicest and kindest people I know. But somehow they had allowed the situation to get under their skin, and their good habits of verbal charity were starting to slip. That morning Jim and Stephanie made a pact over a cup of coffee. They would stop complaining about the imperfect situation and start highlighting in their own minds and to one another the positive qualities of the business partner and his work. They started right away by recalling the reasons Jim went into business with him in the first place. Those reasons hadn't changed. Yes, as a salesman he exaggerated a bit, talked too much, and dramatized everything about the business, but he was a talented man with a great heart, and Jim had made a good decision to go into business with him.

After three weeks of this new resolution, not only were Jim and Stephanie acting more like the Christians they are (a good in itself); they were also seeing immediate benefits on a practical level. The working relationship improved considerably, and my friend and his wife had no more sleepless nights: "Love one another with mutual affection; anticipate one another in showing honor" (Rom. 12:10).

Most of us have been taught not to lie or gossip, and we rightly feel guilty when we fall. But being the hands and feet of Christ in our speech is not only about avoiding saying bad things. We cannot reduce our charity to averting gossip, slander, or calumny. The Christian should stand out for his uplifting words of mercy and kindness in relation to everyone.

Know and Love People for Who They Are

Being the hands and feet of Christ is usually easier with strangers than with people close to home, or in our home. In my years as a priest and counselor I have seen that most in-house relationship difficulties are created because we think we know the other person but we really don't, or because we want them to be what they are not. We wonder why we can't communicate well when the real problem is that we don't know, or are unwilling to accept, who we are communicating with and what makes them tick.

Last year a woman whose marriage was falling apart came to me. I asked her to describe to me the relationship and how it had evolved (devolved). In tears she told me how it had gone from perfect to desperate over a five-year period. They had dated for almost two years and, according to her, never had a single fight in all that time. She said the man she used to know, particularly during their dating years, was warm, attentive, considerate, and very calm. He was now cold, distant, and "completely on the moon." He didn't care what happened to her or the family. The more the marriage deteriorated, the more indifferent he became. After about an hour I asked her if her husband was willing to talk to me. She said he was but that they had decided it would be best for the two of them to be together when he did.

I immediately told her that would not be possible. Since I had already spoken to her alone, the next step would be for me to talk alone with him. She said she completely disagreed with the approach because they really needed to work this out together. She doubted if her husband would even accept the idea of his coming alone. "It's up to you," I said calmly. "Talk it over, and let me know what you decide."

The next day I got a call from Jill saying that to her surprise Matt was willing to come alone. I was available, he could stop over that same day. Never have I met a husband and wife so different one from the other, even on the outside. Whereas Jill was short, thin, and immaculately kept, Jim was tall, pear-shaped, and a bit grizzly. The most striking characteristic of his personality was his slowness. All reactions were delayed; talking to him was like watching a foreign reporter with a slow satellite connection trying to talk to an anchor in New York. His thought process at first seemed belabored, but I soon realized it was deep and sharp . . . just slow.

Jill was right about Matt being on the moon. He was clueless as to why Jill thought things were so bad. "All of a sudden she started flipping out," he said in monotone. "I think she'll be fine, though."

Over the next few weeks my job was to introduce them to each other. It turns out their only marriage problem was that they had never met. Jill assumed Matt was like her, only with attitude problems. Matt knew Jill wasn't like him, but he didn't know why.

Matt was slow because he didn't feel the intensity of emotional impulses that Jill did. Life activities stimulated him at about 20 percent the level they did for Jill. When the kids got sick with seasonal flus, he noticed and he cared, but he didn't feel it. It was seasonal, after all. It happened last year, and it will happen again next year. And if for some reason one of the children got very sick, they would deal with that when it came.

Jill, on the other hand, aware months in advance that the flu season was coming, was waiting for it to strike while hoping it wouldn't happen. When it came, she *felt* terrible. Why didn't those flu shots work?! She hated watching the kids suffer, and she feared the worst.

Why did it take so long for the problem to surface? Prior to their wedding and even in the first years of marriage, the level of importance of their activities seemed relatively inconsequential to Jill. She was selfless and caring. When things didn't work out the way she planned, it mattered, but not that much—because, after all, it was just her. But a few years into the marriage, things started mattering more. Matt's current salary was not going to ensure college educations for the kids. Living in Nebraska meant the kids wouldn't grow up with their cousins. They might never even know their grandparents.

While both Matt and Jill agreed that raising a family meant the stakes in life were now higher, they experienced the same difficult reality in a very different way. Matt *knew* it, and Jill *felt* it.

I told Matt the following: "Remember how you told me Jill all of a sudden starting flipping out when there were problems? Well, believe it or not, that's what she wants to see you do. Jill is an *emotive* person. She needs to *feel* that you care. That's how she can be most sure you mean what you say. If you really want to make her happy, flip out every once in a while."

I told Jill this: "Don't talk to Matt at night about problems. That's when he is slowest; he wants to go to sleep. Wait until the morning. Second, unless you want to get mad, never ask Matt how he *feels* about the problem. Ask him what he *thinks*. Then believe him. Matt cares deeply about each of the family's challenges, but remember, Matt is a *nonemotive* person.

Matt and Jill are doing great. Would that all cases were so simple!

Matt and Jill's road to real connection involved retraining their minds to instinctively make judgments based on their new understanding of how the other worked. Matt began to plan out acts of kindness—yes, plan out!—to express how much he cared. Jill decided to write down on paper why she was upset and review it several times during the day before presenting her concerns to Matt—and never at night.

This might sound a bit unromantic, but for them this type of premeditated behavior adaptation was the most loving gift imaginable. It's what allowed them to be the hands and feet of Christ for one another. It's also what made candlelit dinners and weekends away fun again.

The example I used to explain the idea of knowing and loving people for who they are has to do with marriage. The idea, however, applies to all of our relationships. The only way for us to be the hands and feet of Christ in relationships of any type is by coming to know people and love them for who they are.

Build Perspective Around the Suffering of Others

Building perspective around the suffering of others means defining and approaching my life in relation to everything that surrounds it. Humble people naturally build perspective. Here again, for the rest of us, it requires forming the habit.

That's what my friend Melissa did. The circumstances that motivated her to form the habit were accidental; ours can be intentional. We can make decisions that will help us see what surrounds us.

When her number popped up on my caller ID, I hesitated. I knew it would be another sad update about her unsuccessful job search. Melissa had an MBA from a good university and a stellar career as an executive at various textile companies. About two years prior, some tough personal and professional life experiences caught up with her, and all of a sudden she was unemployed. Because she identified her self-worth disproportionately with what she did, when her employer let her go she almost lost it. She saw it as the ultimate failure for a forty-something single woman.

I took three deep breaths and answered the phone. I heard happiness in her voice! In fact, she was bubbling over with joy. I was a bit curious about where she had landed the job that she must have found to be sounding so cheerful. But strangely enough, she talked to me about everything except work. When she said she had to get going, I was a bit bewildered. *Maybe she wants me to ask,* I thought, so I took the risk. "So how's the job search?" "Oh, not good, but that's OK," she replied quickly. I was silent for a couple of seconds, waiting for her to stop pulling my leg, break down, and tell me the good news. Silence.

I continued: "And why, Melissa, is that all of a sudden OK?" She laughed and said, "I'll tell you next time we talk."

The following week I received a UPS package. In it was a long and beautiful letter from Melissa. Here are a few snippets:

> You asked me why I was happy to be unemployed. I'm not, but as of six weeks ago today, I'm happy to be healthy, to have family, a few great friends, and for all the jobs I've had in the past. . . .
>
> It was a rainy Thursday. I was bored and thoroughly fed up with working the phones among all my old contacts. To break up the day I decided to check out the interior of the newly constructed building down the street—an upscale nursing home.
>
> When the receptionist smiled at me as I walked in the door, I knew I wouldn't be able to mosey around unnoticed, as I had hoped. "Good morning, welcome to Great Lakes. Are you here to see someone, ma'am?" She had a friendly and confident tone.
>
> "No, thank you. I live up the street and was just curious to see how the building turned out."

Miss Sunshine kept probing: "I see, so you don't have a relative here, then?" Some rather unkind thoughts raced through my head about how slow this lady was to catch on.

I answered politely, "No, I don't. I live up the street and was just curious."

She didn't look concerned in the least. "While you are here would you like to visit a resident who doesn't have family members in the area? We are always looking for volunteers."

I'm sure I turned white. Visit someone I don't know? A million excuses bombarded my mind. None of them held water. "Um, sure, I'm really tight on time right now, but if you had someone in particular in mind . . ."

Almost two months later, Father Jonathan, I'm a different person. I'm still without a good job, but that's nothing. I'm embarrassed to think about how much pity I wasted on myself when some of these beautiful people have been all but forgotten by family and friends. My problems seemed so big . . . and to some extent they are to me . . . but nothing in comparison to the real loneliness some of these people, my new friends, endure every day.

Perspective doesn't change everything. It didn't get Melissa a job. It won't get us out of the hospital, bring back our runaway husband or wife, or pay the bills. What it does is level the playing field. When Jesus tells us not to worry because "[m]y grace is sufficient" (2 Cor. 12:9), he is saying he will give us the strength to deal with the real problems at hand, not with what we imagine the problems to be.

The first step in building perspective is to recall conscientiously, or even write down on paper, the good things in life, without adding *but*s. The second is to make note of all of the people who are suffering more than we are. The temptation here is to try to build this perspective with big brushstrokes. A big brushstroke sounds like this: "Yeah, I guess things could be worse. There are people in Africa who don't have food." Unless you've been to Africa and hugged a starving child and cleaned their bed wounds, that kind of big brushstroke just doesn't work. It doesn't change our perspective. In fact, in this case, the thought of faceless African children only makes us feel worse.

Until we've touched someone else's suffering and allowed ourselves to experience *compassion,* it remains an idea—a sad one—and another reason to feel sorry for ourselves.

Reading history—both secular and biblical—is another good way to build perspective. Christians are especially good at complaining: "The world is coming to an end"; God won't be able to put up with modern society any longer!" Too many preachers go down this road, and some even predict the day and the hour of our demise.

A brief glance at almost any other period in history can make us grateful for how good things are today in many parts of the world, materially and even spiritually.

We can recall the life of the biblical character Job for an example of a master perspective builder. You'll remember he's the innocent one whom God tested with every kind of suffering imaginable. The devil was convinced Job worshiped God only because things were going well for him, and he made a bet with God that he could make Job deny his faith, if God would allow him, the devil, to bring calamity upon Job. God took up the offer, probably to teach the rest of us a lesson. Job remained faithful—he didn't curse God. But boy, did he suffer.

> *I loathe my life. I will give myself up to complaint; I will speak*
> *from the bitterness of my soul.*

I will say to God: Do not put me in the wrong! Let me know
*   why you oppose me.*
Is it a pleasure for you to oppress, to spurn the work of your
*   hands, and smile on the plan of the wicked?*

. . . .

Why then did you bring me forth from the womb? I should
*   have died and no eye have seen me.*
I should be as though I had never lived; I should have been
*   taken from the womb to the grave.*
Are not the days of my life few? Let me alone, that I may
*   recover a little*
Before I go whence I shall not return, to the land of darkness
*   and of gloom,*
The black, disordered land where darkness is the only light.
*   (Job 10:1–3, 18–22)*

When *we* say the things Job said, it's usually because we're depressed. But that was not Job's case! He had *every* good reason to want to die. He lost all of his riches overnight, his children died of natural disasters, many of his friends abandoned him, and he himself became deathly sick (Job 1:13–2:13). Then add to all of this the fact that the devil was dedicated full-time to telling him lies about the God in whom he believed.

So why didn't Job curse God, as his wife suggested: "Curse God and die" (Job 2:9)? Because he was a master perspective builder! When he made his list of good things in life, he included *supernatural truths*. His faith was so strong that he believed in God's *unfailing* love for him. Job knew God in a personal way, and because he did, he trusted that his all-loving, all-powerful friend must have a bigger, better plan, even if he himself couldn't see it or even imagine what it could be.

Think Big, Think Smart, Act Now

The final suggestion I would like to offer is to form the habit of thinking big, thinking smart, and acting now.

The world's problems are big, and they demand equally big and effective solutions. I have met so many entrepreneurs who work day and night to make their businesses thrive. The ones who make it are never content with staying afloat; they think outside the box for creative ways to gain a larger share of the market. If we can think big for money, how much more should we think big for building the Kingdom of God! We can complain to our parish priest or pastor about the empty pews, or we can do something about the anti-Christian culture that is the real cause for religious indifference.

Jesus calls us to be in the world but not of the world, to "be shrewd as serpents and simple as doves" (Matt. 10:16), and to "become all things to all. . . . for the sake of the gospel" (1 Cor. 9:22–23). He is telling us to think smart when we think big. He wants us to use our heads, not only our hearts, to spread his message of love and life. He is inviting us to use every ounce of our creative powers and professional training to penetrate the present culture of death and transform it into a culture of life.

Does this sound overwhelming? The culture Jesus calls us to evangelize is big, but it is also small. Yes, it is the megastructures of politics, media, education, and health care, but it is also our family, neighborhood, workplace, and town hall. The best way to think big and think smart is to act now. I know a very wealthy man—a billionaire—who spent his youth and most of his adulthood building his empire. There came a point in his life when he realized that none of this earthly treasure would matter much once he died. He even doubted whether so much wealth would be a true benefit to his kids. What kind of people would they become with everything handed to them on a silver plate?

So he quit making money and started to spend it on others with the intention of dying poor. After several years of philanthropic and charitable work, he realized he had made a mistake. "I started too late," he told me. "I still have money and some great ideas, but my energy is dwindling. I realize now that I would have accomplished much more for these projects, which I consider much more important than any of my businesses, if I hadn't waited so long. I always knew I would spend my golden years on God, but now I wish I would have given him my youth, too."

If we form the habit of regularly speaking well of others, knowing and loving people for who they are, building perspective around the suffering of others, and thinking big, thinking smart, and acting now, we will be worthy hands and feet of the Good Samaritan.

There are still many victims along the side of the road, and many more of us priests and Levites who walk away from their bleeding wounds. What they need are not only better social workers and politicians but, above all, men and women who see with the eyes of Jesus and whose hearts beat in unison with his. Good Samaritans *do* God's work, first and foremost because they know who they *are:* God's children, and coworkers in his redemptive mission.

Questions for Personal
Reflection or Discussion

> ➤ Who needs me to be the hands and feet of Christ for them today?

> ➤ What should be my strategy to be an effective Good Samaritan, given my particular talents and the circumstances of my life?

15

Sketching a Plan for the Spiritual Life

Do you not know that the runners in the stadium all run in the
race, but only one wins the prize? Run so as to win.
Every athlete exercises discipline in every way. They do it to win a
perishable crown, but we an imperishable one.
Thus I do not run aimlessly; I do not fight as if I were
shadowboxing.
No, I drive my body and train it, for fear that, after having
preached to others, I myself should be disqualified.

—I CORINTHIANS 9:24–27

In the simplest of terms, I've described the essence of holiness as union with God. It is not about doing many pious activities, saying long prayers, or even executing virtuous acts. Holiness is a gift from God. It is free and undeserved.

If personal holiness is the fast track to making sense of suffering, and if God gives the undeserved gift of holiness to whomever he wishes, we find ourselves in a mighty fine predicament: there is nothing we can do to get what we need.

Right? Not exactly. There is nothing we can do *on our own* to get the holiness *God wants for us*. But there is plenty we can do to cooperate with God's grace. Our holiness is an essential part of God's Promise, and he asks only that we do our small part to make his plan and purpose flourish.

At different times in the history of the Christian Church, more or less emphasis has been placed on man's cooperation with God's grace for holiness. There have been those who have gone to the extreme of turning holiness into an exercise of the will, a voluntaristic approach that turns God into our own vending machine of grace. Others have looked at our incapacity to merit sanctification and given up all hope on participating in God's project. They have thrown in the towel on spiritual progress with the pretense that holiness is up to God.

I suggest a third route. While the virtuous man is not necessarily the holy man, the holy man is always a virtuous man. He sees all of his faults and misery and still works hard to become more like God. And God never disappoints. The holy man embarks on a quest for perfection not to achieve virtue for its own sake, nor even primarily to get rid of sin, but rather out of love for God and for his neighbor.

This is to say that we have to get to work on holiness. God wants it, and he wants us to do our part: "[W]ork out your salvation with fear and trembling" (Phil. 2:12).

Our fifth principle for freedom-living is sketching a plan for our spiritual life. Politicians labor day and night over their campaign strategies and sometimes even over their policy platforms. Business executives constantly hone their vision statements and their specific plan to beat out their competitors. Athletes work with trainers to develop the perfect diet and exercise routine.

Real professionals leave nothing to chance. They think things through and use every resource at their disposal to get where they want to go. Why, when it comes to holiness, are we so unprofessional? If union with God is our life project, why do we wing it? Sketching a plan for our spiritual life means putting down on paper our personal strategy for cooperating better with God's plan for our holiness.

Here's how to do it:

1. Identify Your Major Obstacle (Your "Root Sin")

Set aside some time to reflect on yourself and, more specifically, on your relationship with God and with others. If I knew I was going to die today, would my conscience be at ease? What are my most typical sins? How do I most hurt others? What is the biggest obstacle between God and me?

The best way to get to know yourself as God knows you is to go beyond the individual faults you commit and try to discover the root causes of your actions. Losing patience, lying, drinking too much, getting angry, or procrastination may seem like our biggest obstacles to holiness, but, in fact, these bad habits are manifestations of something deeper.

We can identify three "root sins" in the spiritual life. They are *pride, vanity,* and *sensuality.* All three of these have some sway on our actions, but in all of us, one of the three is usually dominant. We can say we are mostly proud, vain, or sensual. I am going to define all three. Not everyone whose root sin is pride, for example, will see himself in every part of my description of it, but there will be enough there to identify himself with pride as opposed to vanity or sensuality.

Identifying our "root sin" will give direction to the rest of our work in the personal plan we are sketching for the spiritual life.

PRIDE

The proud person puts himself at the center of his thoughts and priorities. He is self-important and rarely thinks of others first. He has too high an opinion of himself. He is easily annoyed with those who contradict him, is judgmental, and tends to gossip. He is slow to recognize his own mistakes and has a very hard time seeking forgiveness and forgiving others. He knows how things should be and dismisses the suggestions of others without giving them the benefit of the doubt. He is given to anger and impatience. He may say prayers, but he doesn't feel the need for God.

His self-love is easily wounded. He nurses grudges and dislikes and distrusts authority. Because he generally puts himself first, he comes across as indifferent to the needs of others. If he likes the people he is with, he tends to dominate the conversation. If he doesn't like them, he walks away.

VANITY

The vain person is a people pleaser. He is overly concerned about his physical appearance. He hates making mistakes, especially in front of other people. Success drives him. He avoids failure and shame at all cost. Sometimes he avoids making the right decision because he doesn't want people to think badly of him. He either loves attention or shuns it out of fear of failure. Sometimes he stretches the truth.

The vain person is sometimes outgoing and other times shy, because what is most important to him is the opinion of others. Popularity, the right friends, a respectable job, and making good money are high priorities. He is easily discouraged by his failures.

SENSUALITY

The sensual person is lazy and always looks for the easy way out. Comfort is king. He likes to please others, but he prefers to please himself. Too much effort is just not worth it. He is last-minute in everything and rarely sacrifices his comfort level to achieve a goal. The only exception is when the goal promises still more comfort. He is unkempt in his personal appearance and shoddy in his work.

Feelings rule the day for the sensual person. If he wakes up on the wrong side of the bed, others will know it. He often daydreams, with himself at the center. Curiosity always gets the best of him. He acts out on his feelings and passions with no regard for his conscience. His group of friends is usually small, because he sees no use in trying to make new friends if the ones he has now make him happy.

Which of these three "root" sins is most present in your life?

2. Set a Goal

Once we have detected our "root sin" and its most common manifestations, we are in a good position to identify an "opposite virtue" as our immediate goal. Here we must be aware of the frequent temptation to focus our spiritual energy on "getting rid" of our root fault, or any fault. That is a negative approach. Our spiritual work should be in harmony with God's work in our soul, which is always eminently positive. Think of the father figure in the parable of the Prodigal Son. It was precisely the father's forgiveness and mercy that drew his son home and moved him to conversion.

We establish our spiritual goal by selecting the virtue that will most help us to become like Christ. We then work to live that virtue as we see Christ lived it in the Gospel. What follows are a few examples of virtues we could select as they relate to the three root sins. Don't worry about selecting the perfect virtue. We all need to work on many virtues. Our plan for the spiritual life should stay focused on one main virtue, with the intention of updating it over time.

Root Sin	Opposite Virtues (choose one)
Pride	Humility, attitude of service, patience, forgiveness, kindness, obedience to God, generosity, constant concern for others, charity
Vanity	Humility, honesty, principled decision-making, love of God above all things, charity
Sensuality	Tenacity, attitude of service, self-control, purity in our thoughts and actions, moderation, self-sacrifice

3. Identify Threats

What are the major threats to my spiritual life? In particular, what threatens my work toward forging this virtue that God wants for me?

If you have discovered that vanity is your root sin, for example, with a little more reflection you can identify the moments of your day or week where you are tempted to act vainly. I find it helpful to examine the threats in the following three areas: relationship with God; relationship with others; and in my interior. (The examples I give relate to vanity, but a similar list of threats could be made for pride or sensuality.)

RELATIONSHIP WITH GOD

- I forget to take time for prayer because I am self-absorbed.

- I don't seek God's forgiveness because I hate to admit my faults.

- Sometimes I am a traitor to my faith because I am afraid of what people will think.

- I think more about what other people think of me than what God thinks of me.

RELATIONSHIP WITH OTHERS

- I look to be the center of attention in conversations.

- I'm afraid to speak the truth out of fear of what others will think.

- At times I go against my conscience at work because I want my boss's approval.

- I flirt with coworkers in a way I know my spouse would not approve.

IN MY INTERIOR

- My thoughts are centered on my own problems instead of on the needs of those around me.

- I give in to fear of what others think of me.

- I waste time worrying about my external appearance.

- I hold grudges against people who have offended me and am jealous of the good qualities and successes of others.

4. Make a Strategy

Now we are in a position to identify a few simple and realistic actions that will make up our strategy for moving toward our specific spiritual goal. We can use the same three areas we have just listed.

RELATIONSHIP WITH GOD

- I need to begin praying every day. I will use my ride to work to read at least one chapter of the Bible, beginning with the Gospels.

- I will stop what I am doing and ask God for strength and wisdom before beginning any major task during the day.

- I will bring my family to church every Sunday, even when I don't feel like it.

- I will never masquerade my belief in God or pretend I am not religious in front of others out of fear of what they will think.

RELATIONSHIP WITH OTHERS

- I have to start thinking of others first, especially how I can best serve _____, whom I have such a hard time getting along with.

- I will change the conversation when it turns to gossip or character defamation, even when I am embarrassed to do so.

- I will never exaggerate my personal successes or victories.

- I will speak well of others, especially the people at work I am most competitive with, or with whom I don't get along.

IN MY INTERIOR

- I will spend a few minutes before going to bed each evening to review this plan for my spiritual life and evaluate in God's presence how I have done.

- On the way to work, I will make a practical resolution about what I am going to do that day to become more like Christ in my virtue.

- I will try to purify my intention in everything I do. If I am doing something out of vanity instead of out of love for God and others, I will stop and do the right thing.

- I won't try to hide my own weaknesses and limitations from the people around me. Honesty and openness will be my way of life.

Outline for Sketching My Plan for the Spiritual Life

Here is a simple outline you can use to sketch a plan for the spiritual life.

MAJOR OBSTACLE ("MY ROOT SIN")

_____

Manifestations of My Root Sin in Daily Life

I. _____

2. _____

3. _____

SPIRITUAL GOAL ("MY OPPOSITE VIRTUE")

_____

Threats to Attaining This Goal

In my relationship with God

1. _____

2. _____

3. _____

In my relationship with others

1. _____

2. _____

3. _____

In my interior

1. _____

2. _____

3. _____

STRATEGY

In my relationship with God

1. _____

2. _____

3. _____

In my relationship with others

1. _____

2. _____

3. _____

In my interior

1. _____

2. _____

3. _____

How to Use the Outline

If you take the time to sketch this plan for your spiritual life, you will have already have made significant progress. Even if you were never to look back at this personal plan again, preparing it would help you to know yourself better and focus your attention on spiritual goals.

But this plan can give even more. It can become your daily companion as it has become mine. Type out your personal plan in a convenient format, and keep it close to you. Use it as an examination of conscience before you go to bed or as a motivation at the beginning of your workday. If you have a spiritual director or a friend with whom you can share your spiritual goals, review each point with him on a regular basis and ask for guidance on how to be more faithful to the call of God in the nitty-gritty of life's ups and downs.

As you sketch your plan, I suggest you glance back at the first four principles for freedom-living. They should be part of your planning process. They need not appear explicitly in your plan's strategy, but they will certainly influence the way you discern your points of work.

The five principles of freedom-living are a unit and, together with the grace of God, have the power to transform otherwise useless suffering into a means of great sanctification and personal fulfillment. It is a journey of great adventure.

My prayers are with you. Please pray for me.

APPENDIX ONE

Court of Appeals

I will put enmity between you and the woman, and
between your offspring and hers; he will strike at your
head, while you strike at his heel.

—GENESIS 3:15

I don't think there is any worse suffering than the loss of a young child in a tragic accident or to illness. It is also the ultimate test of our faith. Many people suffer terrible physical suffering and, with a little humility, avoid asking "Why me?" or blaming God. But I don't know a single parent who has lost a young child who didn't ask, in one form or another, the classic question we have already referred to many times: "How can an all-loving, all-powerful God allow this to happen?"

Vanessa and Luke went through this. Their three-year-old daughter was kidnapped, abused, and viciously murdered. They will never get over it. They will never completely heal.

Besides the unimaginable and inexplicable emotional pain they went through and still do, Luke and Vanessa suffered spiritually as they looked, apparently in vain, toward God. They needed answers, but initially they came away wondering how he could even exist.

They certainly suffered loneliness on account of Emily's absence, but they eventually experienced another type of loneliness. It was spiritual loneliness owing to God's apparent silence and absence.

In this part of the book I'm going to show you how far we can go—how many answers we can get from the use of logic and faith principles.

We'll be talking directly to Vanessa about her and Luke's journey to hell and back. We begin by confronting the relationship of our suffering and the presence of evil in the world.

As you read along, keep in mind that this fictional conversation takes place five years after Emily's death and that Vanessa is pursuing *intellectual* explanations for what God has to do with suffering, if anything. The answers Dr. Woods gives are not intended to help her heal as a person. They don't pretend to be a remedy for her suffering or even faith explanations to mend a broken soul; rather, they are intended to help her overcome the intellectual barriers that sometimes keep us as sufferers from being open to the spiritual and human journey we have already begun.

Vanessa: Thanks for dinner last night, and for staying so late. Luke and I appreciate all your time. God knows what a tough year it's been, once again.

Dr. Woods: I know, Vanessa. It's true. Who would have thought, ten years ago, things would be this tough today. It seems like yesterday you were heading off on your honeymoon. Remember?

Vanessa: How could I forget—the glory days!

Dr. Woods: In these years you've suffered more than most couples suffer in a lifetime. Your bout with cancer was grueling, but nothing in comparison to the loss of little Emily, and under such circumstances. It's as bad as it gets.

Vanessa: I know. And I wish I could say "That's life" and move on. You know I can't. But anyway, I woke up this morning with something on my mind. I think it was provoked by something you told us last night. You said, if I remember well, "Suffering is a result of evil."

Dr. Woods: Yes, you're astute! Did you disagree?

Vanessa: I don't know. But for some reason it stuck with me. Luke thought I was going crazy when I woke him up this morning at 5 A.M. to ask him what evil means.

Dr. Woods: Let me guess. He said you're evil for waking him up.

Vanessa: No, that's the type of thing he used to say. He's wised up. He just smiled—a semiconscious one—and said we could talk about it in the morning.

Dr. Woods: Oh, yes, a wise man. Did you remind him in the morning?

Vanessa: Yes, but he was in a hurry. So I dusted off our Webster's and had a look myself.

Dr. Woods: And what did it say?

Vanessa: I wrote it down. Let's see: "evil: adjective. morally bad, wicked; harmful, tending to harm; disagreeable."

Dr. Woods: And did that help?

Vanessa: Not at all! I don't want synonyms. I want an explanation.

Dr. Woods: You realize this is a tough question, don't you? Do you really want to talk this out?

Vanessa: Yeah, I do.

Dr. Woods: And why?

Vanessa: Because when I think of evil things, I connect them to evil people. So if suffering is a result of evil, as you said, it means it shouldn't be here, and someone is probably to blame. Does that make sense?

Dr. Woods: Well, yes, it does. I assume beneath your question lies another question. Are you asking, "Is God to blame?" After all, if God is all-powerful, why doesn't he at least stop suffering or keep it at bay?

Vanessa: Well, yes, I guess in the end that's what bugs me. But long ago I decided not to ask that question. It's too painful. I don't want to lose the little faith I have. It's the only thing that keeps Luke and me going.

Dr. Woods: Don't worry. Faith is worthwhile only if it coincides with truth. We can't be afraid to question. I have a feeling God's not offended.

Vanessa: And so? The answer?

Dr. Woods: Not so fast. To find out if God is responsible for evil, either directly or indirectly, it's important to answer your first question about what the essence of evil is. Are you ready?

Vanessa: Yes.

Dr. Woods: I'm going to try to be succinct. Let's start at the beginning. Evil is not a being. We might bump into a villain on the street, but we will never bump into "evil" and shake its hand.

Evil Is Real but Not a Real Thing

Vanessa: What do you mean evil is not a being? What about the guy with red horns and a tail?

Dr. Woods: Well, that's not starting at the beginning. We'll get to him later.

Vanessa: OK, so if evil is not a being, what is it?

Dr. Woods: Evil refers to what's missing, not to what is. Evil is the missing good.

Vanessa: Oh boy, "the missing good"—very philosophical. Do you think you could give me an example?

Dr. Woods: In college I had a pet iguana. Did I ever tell you?

Vanessa: No, you didn't. But I can't stand those animals. Certainly a guy thing!

Dr. Woods: Don't worry. She's long gone. I won't tell you how she died. But I bring her up because we found out the poor thing couldn't fly.

Vanessa: Terrible! Don't tell me. . .

Dr. Woods: It's just an example to show the difference between simply not having and missing. She wasn't missing wings. Iguanas just don't have them. But if, on the other hand, Dorothy—that was her name, by the way—had been born with only three legs, we would say she was missing something. The missing leg would be an evil of sort. Evil is the good that ought to be there but isn't.

Vanessa: OK. But let's keep it simple. Is evil real?

Dr. Woods: Of course! It's real but it's not a real being. Here's an example. Is blindness real?

Vanessa: Obviously.

Dr. Woods: Likewise evil. It's simply the absence of a good that ought to be present—sight, in the case of a blind man.

Vanessa: Now, those examples have to do with material things, but when I think of evil, I think more of people's actions. A really bad deed is evil.

Dr. Woods: Right on. And the same definition applies. An evil action is bad because it is missing goodness. When I lie, I keep people from knowing the truth. When I punch or poison someone, I deprive them of health.

Vanessa: So when you said Luke's and my suffering is a result of evil, what do you mean? I should never have gotten cancer? Emily should never have been killed?

Dr. Woods: Yes, I do mean that.

Vanessa: And so, as I presumed, God is to blame.

Dr. Woods: Blaming God is an easy and almost logical step to take, but if we are going to take it, we should at least know why. And we're not there yet. Before we go on, let's just finish one more point about evil. Believe it or not, it has very much to do both with finding sense in your suffering and with our Christian faith in an all-powerful and all-loving God.

Vanessa: I'm all ears.

Every Evil Has to Hide Out in Some Good

Dr. Woods: No human act is purely evil. Every action—even the most despicable one—is done for the sake of attaining some perceived good.

Vanessa: I'm glad you're not a judge. You know as well as I do some people are flat-out evil and need to spend the rest of their lives in jail!

Dr. Woods: There's no doubt about that. Society has a responsibility to punish bad actions, and even harshly at times. When I say no act is purely evil, I'm talking about something different. Here's an example. When a student cheats on a test, what is he after?

Vanessa: A good grade.

Dr. Woods: Exactly. He's not after the cheating. It's a means to an end, and the end is good.

Vanessa: What about a thief who steals when he doesn't even need the money? I've heard of people like that.

Dr. Woods: I suppose he would be after thrills, good feelings. In every act we seek our happiness in some good. Even the guy who jumps off a skyscraper is not an exception to the rule. In trying to escape despair, he considers death something good. In that sense, he jumps in search of happiness.

Vanessa: I doubt he'll find what he's looking for like that. Can you remind me why we are talking about these melancholic things? I lost my train of thought.

Dr. Woods: The point is that evil always depends on some good to which it clings. We were trying to understand what evil is in order to better understand why it's there.

Vanessa: All that makes sense, but I get the feeling you are saying with fancy words there's really no such thing as evil. What about the guy in red we talked about before: the devil? Is he not a real being?

Dr. Woods: Brilliant. Yes, he is a real being. He's a spirit, a spiritual being. And as long as I say he exists, I surely can't deny the existence of evil, even with fancy words. But even the big guy downstairs is not absolute evil. He's a fallen angel, a creature gone bad. Put goodness where he has put hatred, envy, disobedience, lies, et cetera, and you've got yourself a very different guy.

Vanessa: So you're probably saying evil isn't God's fault because he didn't create it. It's just good that happens to be missing. What a cop-out!

Dr. Woods: Yes and no. I am saying the evil we see in this world is not a creation of God, like you and I are, and those beautiful flowers are. He didn't will evil, and even now he doesn't want it.

Vanessa: But he does permit it. After all, he didn't shield me from cancer or save Emily, and unless he's got one heck of an alibi, I don't need that kind of God.

Dr. Woods: Yes, he does permit it, and we need to know why. But what we've done so far is important. We've clarified terms. Evil is real, but it's not a created being. God is not the cause of evil, but he does permit it.

Vanessa: And I need to know why—a great discussion for another day. I'm not going to let you off easy!

Dr. Woods: I'm sure you won't. We'll talk tomorrow.

Questions for Personal
Reflection or Discussion

➤ How do I understand evil?

➤ Does the idea of evil as a "missing good" rather than part of God's creation help me understand God's role in suffering?

APPENDIX TWO

Earthquakes and Tsunamis

Is God Responsible?

He who made the earth by his power, established the world by his wisdom, and stretched out the heavens by his skill.

—JEREMIAH 10:12

Vanessa: I'm ready to get into it now. I want to know why God permits evil and whether I can hold him responsible.

Dr. Woods: That depends on what kind of evil you mean.

Vanessa: You mean there are different flavors? What kinds of evil are there?

Dr. Woods: There are two main categories: physical evil and moral evil.

Vanessa: What's the difference?

Dr. Woods: Moral evil has to do with things like insulting, lying, and killing. Physical evil has to do with things like earthquakes, sickness, and tsunamis.

Vanessa: Let's take one at a time. I might be able to understand how God isn't responsible for pollution, murder, and war, but who, if not God, is responsible for the droughts and floods that have claimed thousands of innocent human lives, or, getting more personal, for me getting cancer in my first year of marriage?

Dr. Woods: Can I answer your question with a question?

Vanessa: You just did.

Dr. Woods: Why are floods bad?

Vanessa: You tell me.

Dr. Woods: Not because rain is bad. For then why would the drought be evil when rain doesn't fall? Falling rain is not said to be good or bad in itself, but in relation to something else, such as how much is needed for my boysenberries to grow or for my soccer game not to be canceled or for my house to be spared. The flood is bad *for me,* here and now. It is an excess of water in my basement where I keep things *I* value. The drought is bad *for me* because my eggplants aren't going to turn out so good this season.

Vanessa: OK. But let me get something straight. Are you actually trying to say that tsunamis are good?

Dr. Woods: I'm inviting you to take a look at the big picture. Ask the environmental experts, and they will tell you that such natural occurrences are good and necessary in order to replenish the soil, purge certain noxious buildups, relieve tension in the earth's inner plates, and all sorts of beneficial results that have to do with microbes and symbiosis and other things people who subscribe to *Nature* magazine go crazy about, but are way over my head.

Vanessa: But come on, Doctor, be honest. Do you really think that solves the problem?

Dr. Woods: In part.

Vanessa: A very small part! The other part is how all that physical evil—as you call it—affects us creatures. When a giraffe gobbles up some treetops, the giraffe gets something good, but the trees get the short end of the stick. Or when a volcano incinerates an inhabited valley, the volcano is happy to have cleared its throat, but the valley and all its inhabitants are destroyed. Do you remember Pompeii? I'd hardly call that good.

Dr. Woods: I totally agree with you. Do you think, then, that physical evil in general—I mean, the constant interplay of constructive and destructive natural forces, including in our own bodies—fits into a good world?

Vanessa: I can't imagine a world without such forces. What would become of the circle of life? How could there be change?

Dr. Woods: I think a world that couldn't grow or shrink would probably be pretty dull. It would be totally static. The problem, as you said, is when the change makes us suffer.

Vanessa: To tell you the truth, it kind of gets me angry with God. How could he do that to us? And isn't he supposed to be all-loving and all-powerful? Then why does he make his own children suffer?

Dr. Woods: So you think we should put God on trial? Should we order him to justify himself before our tribunal? Should we subpoena God?

Vanessa: Haven't you ever wanted to?

Dr. Woods: You bet. And so have others. Does the name Pontius Pilot ring a bell? He put Jesus on trial.

Vanessa: Let's not go there. It's assuming too much. You're going to ask me to take a leap of faith. You know I'm spiritual, but I'm not willing to be a Jesus freak.

Dr. Woods: Sometimes it's reasonable to take a leap. A real act of faith, in my opinion, is not a blind jump into the darkness, but a reasonable jump into the light.

Vanessa: I guess I'll have to be the judge of that. So why do you think God's not to blame for the suffering that this physical evil, as you call it, causes?

Physical Evil and God's Original Plan

Dr. Woods: It has to do with where suffering came from. Christianity teaches that before original sin entered the world by the disobedience of our first parents, suffering didn't happen.

Vanessa: You're talking about Adam and Eve?

Dr. Woods: Right. God created mankind in a state of original justice and holiness by which we would not have to suffer or die so long as we stayed in God's intimate friendship. In God's original plan for the human race, therefore, mankind was meant to live in harmony with the forces of nature, and not to suffer because of them. At the same time, God gave humanity the gift of intellect and freedom, to choose between right and wrong. The Bible tells us our first parents were too proud to have it God's way (Gen. 3:6). They wanted it their way or no way. They wanted to eliminate the difference between God and themselves.

Vanessa: I don't buy the Adam and Eve story. First parents—maybe—but "God made the world in six days and on the seventh he rested"? Yeah, right. And the apple? Whatever!

Dr. Woods: I know what you mean. I think it is helpful to keep in mind that the book of Genesis is the story of creation. It is not a play-by-play account of a Pittsburgh Steelers game. Six days may mean six thousand years, or six nanoseconds, or something in between. Likewise, the apple may be symbolic, but it's symbolic of something that really happened. Man and woman wanted it their way, even if that way was imperfect.

Vanessa: And things haven't changed too much. Remember the song?

Dr. Woods: How could I forget? "I did it my way."

Vanessa: Sorry for being such a skeptic, but you're assuming a little too much. How would our first parents' rejection of God's plan alter the earth's plates? I sin against God all the time and I've never caused an earthquake.

Dr. Woods: I know what you mean, but your experience is based on a world already out of whack. When Adam and Eve used the gift of their free will to knock God off the cart and take the reins into their own hands, God loved them so much he respected their decision. They didn't want things perfect, and this is what they got. Take a look here at the book of Genesis. The author puts it like this.

To the man he said: "Because you listened to your wife and ate from the tree of which I had forbidden you to eat, Cursed be the ground because of you! In toil shall you eat its yield all the days of your life.

"Thorns and thistles shall it bring forth to you, as you eat of the plants of the field." (Gen. 3:17–18)

Back to Harmony

Vanessa: OK, I can swallow that . . . if not the Bible passage, at least the concept. Let's go back to living in harmony with nature, before the first sin. You are saying God created a perfect world. What about pre-Fall mosquitoes—did they never bite in Eden, or what? Did they never buzz in Adam's ear and annoy him? Did cancer cells just hang out without wreaking havoc, as they did to me?

Dr. Woods: I'm not sure.

Vanessa: And were there volcanoes in Eden? Did liquid rock not burn man's skin back then? Or did flowing magma conveniently sidestep Adam and Eve by some divine plan? Could Adam surf barefoot on lava? Did fluids not flow by the path of least resistance in those days? Or were their bodies exempt from the physical laws ours are subject to?

Dr. Woods: I don't know, Vanessa.

Vanessa: Perhaps Adam and Eve didn't feel. No nerve endings?

Dr. Woods: I wish I could give you the "untold story" about life in Eden, but obviously I can't. But if you insist on getting into particulars, I will agree to speculate so long as we understand that it's just speculation.

Vanessa: Sounds good.

Dr. Woods: We can wonder if the laws of nature were different before the Fall, or if God somehow intervened and kept man from suffering its movements. Maybe it was a combination of both. I suppose if Adam and Eve could sense pain, they sensed it in a very different way, so that they didn't suffer it. Strange as it might be, it's not contradictory to think that a mosquito bite could be almost enjoyable in a different kind of world.

Vanessa: Hmmm . . . a novel thought, for sure.

Dr. Woods: And as for the natural disasters, like volcanoes and earthquakes, I can't imagine how Adam and Eve could have survived them standing up. Perhaps before the Fall, either God prevented earthquakes from striking altogether or else humanity's purer intellect, unstained by sin, allowed people to steer clear of the earth's fault lines.

Vanessa: Well, like you said, it is just speculation.

A Perfect World Wouldn't
Be So Perfect . . .

Dr. Woods: But here's something that's not just guesswork. Sure, nature presents itself as less than ideal, but it seems to me that that's not wholly wrong. If we stop and think a second about what nature is, we see there has to be a certain kind of imperfection in creation. Isn't God the only one who is truly perfect?

Vanessa: So they say.

Dr. Woods: And so when he creates a world of finite, limited beings who are dependent on him and inferior to him, obviously they cannot be as perfect as he is, right?

Vanessa: That makes sense. I remember hearing "Every cause is greater than its effect." Or in modern terms we might say that no computer is smarter than its programmer.

Dr. Woods: Then, creation was never supposed to be equal to God. Paradise was perfectly harmonious and benevolent to man, but it was never absolutely perfect, as God is perfect. Does this make sense?

Vanessa: Yeah . . . actually no, Doctor, it doesn't make sense. Not totally. I have no problem chalking up imperfect things like rotten eggs and dirty laundry to an imperfect world or even to Adam and Eve, but how about atomic bombs, slavery, and child abuse? God can't be off the hook just because two people in a garden sinned.

Dr. Woods: Vanessa, I know that's what hurts most. But so far we've just covered what I called *physical evil.* You just brought up another point, and it has to do with the second kind of evil: *moral evil,* including the evil act of Emily's murder. But maybe we should leave that for tomorrow.

Vanessa: Don't worry. I've got plenty to think about for tonight. I'm sure it's just what Luke wants to hear about when he gets home from work, or when we're going to bed, or when I wake him in the middle of the night! I must say, though, I do find it helpful to imagine a world before the Fall—before anyone ever said to God, "I want it my way." That's the kind of world I could imagine God would create. And the fact that God permits physical evil makes some sense. There've got to be consequences to our actions, both individually and as a human race. It's almost as if God withheld his power—even though he knew we would suffer—to save us from a much greater suffering: the inability to choose freely.

Dr. Woods: I think that's a good way to put it. In that sense God is responsible for the effects of physical evil—the missing harmony in creation—because he permitted it, but he's not its original cause. We were the ones who messed things up. He permits this type of evil because stopping it would in some way be limiting our free will, our capacity for self-determination. Imagine if God performed a disappearing act of every bad consequence of every one of our bad decisions. Would that be real freedom?

Vanessa: Of course not. But when I think of Emily, this all sounds like theory.

Dr. Woods: I know it does. What do you say we talk about that tomorrow?

Vanessa: Let's do it.

Questions for Personal Reflection or Discussion

➤ Was physical evil part of God's original plan? Why does he permit it now?

➤ What's the difference between physical evil and moral evil?

Moral Evil, the Wicked Kind

And the Painful, Logical Consequences of Misused Freedom

When the Lord saw how great was man's wickedness on earth, and how no desire that his heart conceived was ever anything but evil, he regretted that he had made man on the earth, and his heart was grieved.

—GENESIS 6:5–6

Vanessa: These coffee meetings are great. If the other Starbucks junkies only knew that right here at this table we are solving the world's problems.

Dr. Woods: I wish it were that easy.

Vanessa: Well, at least we're having a crack at it. Defining evil as the absence of something good—not something God created—as you've done, and seeing the physical imperfections of this world—the ones that make us suffer—as the result of a perfect plan interrupted by our wish to have things our way, has already helped me confront my problems and those of others in a less cynical way. It makes me a bit less bitter, especially about my cancer. But that's not to say I don't still blame God. I'm still convinced he's either not all-powerful or not all good. Otherwise, one thing is for sure: our little Emily would still be here.

Dr. Woods: If at this point you had everything figured out, I would be a bit concerned. We've still got a ways to go. In fact, we were about to talk about moral evil. Are you ready?

Vanessa: Yep. If nothing else, we will have gotten a caramel latte out of this deal.

Dr. Woods: You are always asking for examples, so I want to start off with that of a gun.

Vanessa: A rather aggressive, start, Doctor.

Dr. Woods: Actually, that's the point. Is a gun evil or is it good?

Vanessa: I suppose you would say it's evil.

Dr. Woods: Nope, at least not how I see it. If a gun shoots straight, if we can hit a target with it, we call it a good gun, and we compliment a marksman for a good shot. The gun is good in itself.

Vanessa: Hmmm, that makes sense. But we must associate evil with the gun for some valid reason.

Dr. Woods: People don't always use guns well. To shoot to murder the innocent is evil, but the evil of such an action is in the human will, not in the bullet. That's why Augustine of Hippo, one of the early Christian bishops, defines moral evil as *disordered love,* nonconformity of man's will to God's will.

Vanessa: So that's where evil is: in the human will?

Dr. Woods: Exactly. Moral evil flows from our will, and we can't exactly blame God for that, right?

Moral Evil Is Disordered Love

Vanessa: I agree, but I'm a bit bewildered. I thought you said evil was the "missing good." Now you say it's disordered love. Which is it?

Dr. Woods: In the case of moral evil, in fact, it's both. Moral evil is the absence of something good that ought to be present—good choices. Of all God's creatures, only angels and people have the capacity to make free choices; everything else is governed entirely by physical or biological laws—like gravity and instinct.

Vanessa: What's your point?

Dr. Woods: Sin—doing morally bad things—is linked to free-dom. Gerbils don't have free will. That's why we don't give them a ticket when they make a mess on the carpet. Bears don't go to jail when they vandalize a picnic area. Man, on the other hand, is dif-ferent. His Creator has endowed him with liberty so that he would have the capacity to love. Without freedom there is no real love.

Vanessa: You mean no true friendship is coerced?

Dr. Woods: Exactly. Even if you put serious psychological pres-sure on Luke to bring you flowers, what makes it so nice when he does is that you know he didn't have to do it. Sound familiar? "You didn't have to do that, Luke."

Vanessa: OK, I think I know where you are going here. When I see people do bad things to innocent people, I wonder why God doesn't stop it. You're saying here, though, that the only way we could possibly love is if we were also free to do bad things—or, as you would probably put it, free to sin. God doesn't stop it, because he would also be stopping our capacity to love.

Dr. Woods: That's it, Vanessa. It's pretty deep isn't it?

Vanessa: But I think I would gladly trade the ability to love for the possibility of a world free of sin. In this case, I would have my daughter back.

Dr. Woods: I know what you mean, Vanessa. But you say you would make the trade precisely because your love for Emily was worth so much. Try to picture for a second our life without the ability to choose. It's what makes us who we are. And knowing all the moral evil that would flow from our twisted hearts, God cre-ated us just the same. He thought love was that good!

Vanessa: So God created us to love, to love him and others, but we messed it up. God's plan failed.

Dr. Woods: In one sense you're right. It did fail. But that's why Jesus died on the cross—it was his way of reconciling his original plan by bridging the gap of our willful separation from him.

Vanessa: You know, I'm not so sure about all of that Jesus stuff, Doctor, even though publicly I'm afraid to admit it. But I do understand how we humans are the cause of evil, and the suffering that comes with it. The first sin shattered the original harmony between mankind and creation. Future sins—moral evil—are the cause of all other pain and suffering.

Dr. Woods: Yes, just think of all the misery brought about by greed, lust, anger, laziness, pride, envy, and gluttony. Evil choices give rise to war, injustice, slavery, abuse, oppression, betrayal, neglect, infidelity, and despair. And as you know well, it was the choice of a very bad man that ended Emily's life.

God's Permissive Will

Vanessa: There's still a big gap.

Dr. Woods: Where?

Vanessa: Even if it is ultimately our fault, the Big Guy lets it happen.

Dr. Woods: Vanessa, you bring back a great point. God doesn't cause evil; he permits it. He lets it happen. I find it helpful to call it his *permissive* or *passive* will. While God makes good things happen—his *active* will—God doesn't make cars crash or babies die. He only allows it to happen.

Vanessa: That wasn't my point. It's helpful to know God doesn't drop the boom on anyone. But as helpful as it is, it still isn't enough. Why does he *let* the boom drop? Are we to believe that the Almighty couldn't stop suffering it he so wished? Couldn't he put an end to the negative effects of an imperfect world or even of our own bad choices, or those of others? Wouldn't that be real love?

Dr. Woods: So it would seem. Although that would be a very strange world, nothing like the one we know now. If God were to intervene and stop the effects of selfish choices or even the effects of a disordered world, would we be truly free human beings? Are we willing to give up our humanity, especially the ability to love and be loved in an imperfect world, so that we may never suffer?

Vanessa: I know, I know . . . but for all of that, it still doesn't explain completely Emily's death, because, yes, I would even trade this world, as we know it, and my ability to choose freely, if I could have her back.

Dr. Woods: But, Vanessa, it is precisely because you *are* free that you can love her so much.

Vanessa: OK. Let's try something else. You think with logic, but life is not all about that. What does God have to say about Emily? Was her death just a logical consequence of the order of things? And Emily is just one example. What about the suffering of the innocent all over this crazy world. Logically—and that's what you seem to be all about—I would have to say God is rather cruel. Be honest: Wouldn't you agree?

Dr. Woods: I would agree, unless, of course, God could bring forth from the evil he permits—even Emily's death—even a greater good than the original good that is now missing, and if he could do this in every instance of evil.

Vanessa: Doctor, what are you saying? What good could come from the death of my child?

Dr. Woods: To be honest, I don't know for sure. But I think God does, and he gives us good hints.

Vanessa and Dr. Woods bring us to the Promise. God's response to human suffering is to bring good out of evil, and to do this always and everywhere, and in the best way for each of us. In chapter 6 we tried to count some of the goods, human and spiritual, that God brings out of our suffering. The humble person willing to see with the eyes of God can find and will marvel at innumerable blessings that come forth from every unfortunate circumstance.

Yet as hard as we look, and with as much faith as one may have, who would dare to try to calculate the greater good from Vanessa and Luke's story? Nobody in their right mind!

The Promise can't be measured or calculated. Our minds are too little, our hearts too small. Perhaps we can't "get it," but we can catch it. We can experience the serenity and joy that come from God's perfect plan taking root in our lives. Parts 2 and 3 of this book have shown us how. They invite us to leave human rationalizations behind and enter into the great adventure of being part of God's response to human suffering.

Questions for Personal Reflection or Discussion

➤ What is the connection between evil and freedom?

➤ Have I ever misused my freedom, becoming the cause of evil for someone else?